Joe

Who Killed Donté Manning?

Peace & All Good.
Thanks for the
companionship.

J Rose
Oct 2012

Advance Praise

"Who Killed Donte Manning? is a poet's detective prose. It's evidence made visible. It's about people who stand before altars seeking answers to their prayers."
E. Ethelbert Miller
Director, African American Resource Center
Howard University

"Berger engages in the ancient prophetic tradition of calling us to bear witness to the 'terrible beauty' of the sacred breaking into our ordinary lives, allowing it to transform ourselves and our communities."
Mirabai Starr
Writer, Translator, Speaker, and Teacher

"Berger's gift for poetic expression shines through each page of this meditation."
Joseph Nangle, OFM
Member of the Assisi Community
Washington, D.C.

"The blood on {Berger's} sidewalk is at once a sacramental grief and a way into the shadows of global economy. Begin with the death of a child and pan back to see the very figure of empire."
Bill Wylie-Kellermann
Pastor, St. Peter's Episcopal Church
Detroit, MI

Who Killed Donte Manning?

The Story of an American Neighborhood

Rose Marie Berger

Apprentice House
Baltimore, Maryland

Library of Congress Cataloging-in-Publication Data

Berger, Rose Marie, 1963-
Who killed Donte Manning? : The Story of an American neighborhood
/ Rose Marie Berger. -- 1st ed.
p. cm.
Includes bibliographical references (p.   ).
ISBN 978-1-934074-40-4
1. Christian sociology--Washington (D.C.) 2. Columbia Heights
(Washington, D.C.)--Social conditions. 3. Manning, Donte Ernest, d.
2005--Death and burial. 4. Cities and town--Biblical teaching. I. Title.
BR560.W35B47 2009
261'.1--dc22
2009006726

Printed in the United States of America
First Edition

Map by Jackie Spycher (2008)
Author photograph by Rick Reinhard
Cover design by Gregg Wilhelm

Published by Apprentice House
The Future of Publishing…Today!

Apprentice House
Communication Department
Loyola University Maryland
4501 N. Charles Street
Baltimore, MD 21210
410.617.5265
www.ApprenticeHouse.com

To my family, the Christian community at Sojourners, and
the people of Columbia Heights in Washington, D.C.

In memory of Donte Ernest Manning

Table of Contents

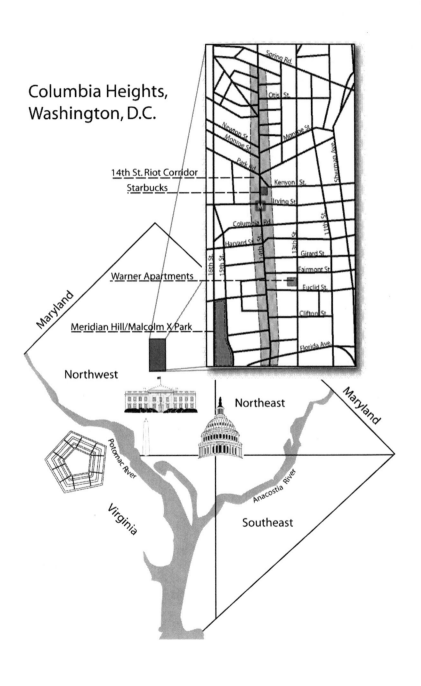

Columbia Heights,
Washington, D.C.

Spring Rd.

Otis St.

Newton St.
Monroe St.

Monroe St.

Sherman Ave.

Park Rd.

14th St. Riot Corridor
Starbucks

Kenyon St.

Irving St.

M

Columbia Rd.

11th St.

Harvard St.

12th St.

14th St.

13th St.

Girard St.

Fairmont St.

Warner Apartments

14th St.

15th St.

Euclid St.

Clifton St.

Meridian Hill/Malcolm X Park

Florida Ave.

Maryland

Northwest

Northeast

Maryland

Potomac River

Anacostia River

Virginia

Southeast

Who Killed Donte Manning?
The Story of an American Neighborhood

"America has never been an empire. We may be the only great power in history that had the chance, and refused—preferring greatness to power and justice to glory."

—Gov. George W. Bush (1999) [1]

"We're an empire now, and when we act, we create our own reality."

—a senior adviser to President George W. Bush (2004) [2]

"We Americans are full of our sense of ourselves as having benign imperial impulses. ... We'd do better in other words if we had a more complicated notion of what the Roman Empire was. We must reckon with imperial power as it is felt by people at the bottom."

—James Carroll, author of Constantine's Sword [3]

Foreword by Jim Wallis

Rose Marie Berger has written a biblical essay on the neighborhood where she lives. I know the neighborhood well, because I lived there too. Her provocative discourse is a theological reflection on "place," which is a long-standing tradition in the Christian faith—a faith that is all about incarnation, the Word becoming flesh in place and time.

The particular "place" where this story begins is in northwest Washington, D.C., on 13th Street between Euclid and Fairmont, on the sidewalk in front of the notorious Warner Apartments where a third-grade boy named Donte Manning was caught in a crossfire of bullets and killed.

Rose lives around the corner from the place where little Donte was shot; I lived right across the street. I remember it well and reading her account of it reminded me of an earlier incident on that same sidewalk many years earlier.

In 1993, the new First Lady had come to Washington. Hillary Rodham Clinton had invited a small group of people to her office at the White House to talk about the growing tragedy of youth violence in our cities, a situation of great concern to her. It was the first time I met Hillary Clinton. The meeting had an assortment of civil rights and religious leaders, urban and community activists, and heads of national organizations that cared about children at risk. I was impressed with Clinton's understanding of the issues, her thoughtfulness and probing questions, and her clear desire to do something that would begin to address the problem.

When the meeting was finished, I came home to my house on 13th Street NW in Columbia Heights ... to lots of yellow tape. Of course, I knew what yellow tape meant: Another crime had been committed here and the scene had been cordoned off by police. I learned that during the very hour we were meeting at the White House to discuss the problems of youth homicide, a young kid had been killed across the street from my house—on the sidewalk in front of the Warner Apartments.

I recall wondering at the time how many of the other participants in that meeting came home to yellow tape. It's not that you know all the answers more easily just because you live there. It's just that place yields perspective.

It is that biblical insight Rose illustrates in the story *Who Killed Donte Manning?*, a story that begins with yet another youth homicide on the 2600 block of 13th Street NW in Washington, D.C. Her biblical reflections on her place, and mine, stretch from Genesis to Revelation, and from Washington, D.C., to the coca fields of Colombia in South America. They describe what happens at the center of "empire" and the consequences at empire's margins, which, in our city and neighborhood, is a journey of only about 2 miles.

Rose writes, "In Washington, D.C., I sometimes feel like I'm walking in the living narrative of the gospels, some kind of time-warped virtual reality. When I want to see live gospel stories, I go to the Amoco (now BP) station at 14th and Euclid."

Reading *Who Killed Donte Manning?* reconnected me both to my own neighborhood and to a biblical interpretation of it that puts the place where Rose and I live into perspective again. And that's always what the theology of incarnation is supposed to do.

•••

Jim Wallis is a founder of Sojourners, a progressive Christian non-profit organization, and editor-in-chief of Sojourners *magazine. His most recent book is* Rediscovering Values: A Moral Compass for the New Economy.

Preface

We are always entering paradise but only for a moment.
—W. H. Auden[4]

When I moved to the riot-dismembered neighborhood of Columbia Heights, Washington, D.C., in 1986, I had no idea I would still be here more than 20 years later. I anticipated a rather bohemian life of Christian itinerancy—owning little property and moving where the spirit led. Instead, I was provided with a 100-year-old house (with much of the original wiring) and the gift of stability.

I've probably traveled more from this neighborhood and from within this neighborhood than I ever would have in my Jesus-version of being a Dharma bum. In Columbia Heights, amid the insecurity, litter, the harshness of poverty and violence of wealth, in the heart of the American Empire, I've entered moments of paradise.

This book was written mostly at home in a house that sits on land that was once part of a large estate at the turn of the 19th century. The first owners of the house, the Cowells, were a white middle-class couple who worked as a stenographer and editor, and rented out rooms in the 1920s to Russian Jewish immigrants. The next householders were a middle-class African-American couple. Mrs. Valentine worked as a real estate agent and her husband was a messenger for the National Geographic Society. The Valentines also took in renters in the 1930s and '40s—Howard University college students, school teachers. In the early 1970s the house was bought by a real estate company. With no human householder to care for it and carry its story, the house faltered and fell into disrepair.

In the late 1970s, the real estate company sold my house to the Sojourners Community—a lay Christian group of political activists dedicated to modeling their lives on the early Christian communities described in Acts 2 and 4. Those first-century Christians were radicals. "They devoted themselves to the teaching of the apostles and to the communal life, to the breaking of the bread and to the prayers," it says in Acts. "All who believed were together and had all things in common; they would sell their property and possessions and divide them among all according to each one's need. …And every day the Lord added to their number those who were being saved" (Acts 2:42-47).

Like many religious communities before it, members of Sojourners withdrew from their places of private comfort and sought to live, work, and minister in the unloved and uncared for places of the world—in this case, the neighborhood of Columbia Heights, heart of Washington, D.C.'s urban poverty.

I moved from California in 1986 to join Sojourners Community. After living in two of the community's houses, I moved into this house in the early 1990s, when it was a part of Sojourners Housing Cooperative. It was from Sojourners that I, along with my co-owner Julie Polter, purchased the house in 2000.

Since the time when Sojourners first aquired it, this house has sheltered homeless mothers, Chicano activists, a tie-dye business, jazz musicians, poets and memoirists, a huge extended family, magazine editors, hunger fasters and dissident farmers, a Kenyan office worker and a Tanzanian bank teller, plus a few dogs and an occasional bird.

It is from this house that, on some mornings, I glimpse little neighborhood boys on their way to school. Donte Manning was undoubtedly one of those boys—laughing with the school crossing guard, running with his friends, scraping handfuls of snow off parked cars for snowballs. He was just a little boy.

In the mysterious mechanics of God's universe, Donte's murder around the corner from my house on Holy Thursday in 2005 set off a spiritual alarm deep inside me. I followed the scraps of his story in *The Washington Post*.

I read the police reports and spoke with neighbors. Over time, his story became linked with my own—and, through this writing, with our own story as Americans.

Our American story includes the overt transformation in our own lifetime from America as a flawed ideal of a democratic republic to an America defined from the highest quarters of power as an empire. An empire is a government or business that has expanded its territory or economic control over populations distinct from itself by use of force. Empires have traditionally been antithetical to democratic republics. Biblically, empires—Egypt, Babylon, Rome—are antithetical to God's liberating spirit. What questions does this raise for people of faith in America today?

The base Christian communities in Latin America and the global South teach that our perspective is shaped by what we see out the window every morning when we wake up. *Who Killed Donte Manning?* reflects, in part, what I see, and our shared vision, I think, of what you might see.

Rose Marie Berger, Washington, D.C.
Feast of St. Barbara

Chapter 1
Outlining the Body of a City

But when I die, I'ma be so high
that I'ma get up and walk, leavin the concrete bare
with the chalk outline still there.
—Hip hop artist Eminem, "Hellbound" [5]

Donte Manning was in the third grade when he was shot in the face around the corner from my house in 2005. Pop, pop, pop. It was Holy Thursday—a little before 10 p.m. The next morning I was leaving Washington, D.C., for a trip to El Salvador. Pop, pop, pop. Six shots on a street filled with kids enjoying a warm night before the Easter holiday.

The bullets left 9-year-old Donte in a coma. A month later, his family decided to take him off life support. "It was a decision the family made with some agony," District police captain C.V. Morris said. Donte survived four more days. I learned that he'd died over our neighborhood e-mail list. "Ervin20010 has sent you a story," the subject heading read. "NBC4.com - News - 9-Year-Old Shooting Victim Dies." He died on the feast of St. Paschasius Radbertus—a Tuesday in the fifth week of Easter.

I couldn't escape the inexorable way that Donte's shooting and death followed the Christian liturgical calendar. As a poet, I'm interested in images and rhythms. I notice the effect they have on us as human beings. We develop certain filters to process the images and rhythms surrounding us. Those filters are our mythologies, symbologies, theologies, cosmologies. They are grand, over-arching narratives that shape the world view of an individual or society and give meaning. They are our religion.

Here are two images. Paschasius Radbertus wrote in 831 the first treatise on the Eucharist, titled *De Corpore et Sanguine Domini* (*The Body and Blood of the Lord*). In theologian Shane Rosenthal's article "Radbertus & Ratramnus: Ninth Century Debate Over the Lord's Supper" he writes, "Radbertus ... identified the eucharistic body as that of the exact same historical body of Christ, and he asserted that this body was placed in the believer's mouth [during communion] in reality, and not merely symbolically." [6] I juxtapose Radbertus' image of the "real Presence" of Christ against a photo *The Washington Post* published of 8-year-old Fidel Maldonado, Donte's next-door neighbor, as he watched D.C. police pull bullets out of parked cars. The newspaper had cropped out of the original photo police scrubbing Donte's blood off the sidewalk.

"The Spirit from the substance of bread and wine daily creates the flesh and blood of Christ by invisible power," wrote Radbertus.[7] Real bodies. Real blood. The tension between the images allows interpretive space where the ancient and the immediate can meet, where theological questions can be grounded in tradition and yet address real life.

Cities are not the only place this can happen, but in cities—where images are shoved against each other in tight quarters—the interpretive space is more recognizable. In the history of Judeo-Christian imagination the city has represented many things. The Hebrew scriptures tell the stories of the earliest human settlements; the Christian gospels portray Jesus' Jerusalem; and the Book of Revelation is constructed around an image of the "City of God." How do these biblical images of the city theologically interrogate "my" city of Washington, D.C., and my neighborhood of Columbia Heights? How can urban space be read as biblical narrative?

Maybe the most important question any of us— especially Christians with our belief in incarnation—can ask is: Where are the bodies in a city? Where do people locate themselves temporally, spatially, and spiritually? Who lives, who dies, and why? Whose blood is sacrificed on whose altar and for what purpose? Is Donte's blood—shed on this city sidewalk—also Christ's blood? Doctrinal and theological arguments aside, everything in me says yes: Christ's blood and Donte's blood are intimately connected because the cross is always in relationship with the least and the lost.

To recognize and engage interpretive space requires, among other things, a more than passing knowledge of history. One needs intimate knowledge of one's location and a pre-modern sense of time. The early Christian monks met these requirements first by taking a "vow of stability," as St. Benedict put it (a commitment to live in a particular monastic community for life) and, second, by observing the Liturgy of the Hours (a set of prayers said at certain times every day) and the liturgical year (the annual cycle of seasons such as Advent, Christmas, Epiphany, Lent, Easter, and Pentecost).

In contemporary urban settings one needs knowledge of the bioregion, history, and demographics of where one lives—as well as really getting to know the neighbors and their histories. Developing an alternate sense of time in modern urban settings is more difficult, but it is possible if you follow the church calendar or are accustomed, like many Pentecostals, charismatics, or Holiness members, to the kairotic, unexpected, inbreaking of the Spirit—

disrupting our normal chronotic, sequential experience.

•••

How do I engage the interpretive space outside my row house window? Let's start with some history. The house I live in was built in 1901. At that time, "Columbia Heights was still half unpaved, a brand new development being touted as a pastoral escape from the city—affluent and elite, meant for whites only," writes magazine editor and Columbia Heights resident Julie Polter in her essay "On the Heights.""Since then the neighborhood has gone from being suburb to inner city to a rapidly gentrifying hot spot, with oft-shifting demographics of race, class, and income that those original developers couldn't have imagined." [8]

In 1986, when I moved to Columbia Heights, it was only on the cusp of surviving. The 1968 "riot corridor" pierced 14th Street—the heart of the neighborhood's Black-owned business district. In 1990, Columbia Heights led the District of Columbia—which led the nation—in numbers of murders committed. [9]

The Warner Apartments at 2620 13th Street—where Donte Manning lived—were built by the Kennedy & Davis development company around 1920 in the architectural style known as Colonial Revival. [10] In the same era, Kennedy

& Davis also built the block of five row houses across the street.[11]

Fran and Larry Bellinger live in one of those houses. Fran, a former judge, has multiple sclerosis and is a passionate quilter in the tradition of the African-American slave and story quilts. Larry is a writer, political organizer, occasional tour guide, and bank officer. "The night Donte was shot," Larry told me, "I was watching the NCAA playoffs and Fran was upstairs working on a quilt. I heard several shots in rapid succession and then a lot of screaming. I went to the front windows with cell phone in hand dialing 9-1-1 while I ran.

"I was looking out of the window when I was jarred by the sight of the people reacting to the incident. That they were running back and forth, jumping up and down and screaming was not unusual. I have seen that scenario played out in other times in other places ... but that's when I realized they were all children, not even in their teens. By then Fran had come downstairs and was crying, 'It's a little boy!'"[12]

Fran and Larry learned Donte had been taken to Children's Hospital and was still alive. Fran, who serves on the hospital board, decided to make a quilt for him. "Most kids come to Children's for medical procedures and treatment," said Fran, "but many are brought in as victims.

When a child has been molested or assaulted and brought into Children's, their clothes are taken for evidence. They are given blankets to wrap up in and hold onto. The blankets provide a tactile source of comfort for victimized children."[13]

Fran chose a fabric with an animal pattern she hoped would delight a child. The reverse side had a pattern of African masks. "I wanted to represent the solidarity of the neighborhood in support of the Manning family," Fran said. After Donte died Fran gave the quilt to Donte's mother.

•••

While I am reading the interpretive space of Columbia Heights historically, I'm also reading it as a Christian and from within a culture steeped in Judeo-Christian imagery. With this double vision, I'm tracking a number of biblical images of the city—trying to uncover the "Ur" in urban.

But my primary search is for the location of the altar. Where are the sacrifices made? Where is blood offered or taken? The Genesis creation story reveals that in Eden, there was no altar. In the "dream time" described in the book of Genesis, humans were part of a natural symbiotic system created by God. The social, environmental, and spiritual realms operated in mutually advantageous ways. Therefore, an altar of sacrifice was not needed. One did not need to plead for one's life. Everything was given. Everything was gift. The "economy" was not rooted in chattel or capital. It functioned by cooperative relationship. It was in balance, organic, "erotic" as essayist Lewis Hyde describes it in his book *The Gift*.[14] It was abundant, prolific, and fertile. It did not presume a scarcity model.

Cities came later. Cities are a result of the Fall and exile from Eden. In the Hebrew narrative, cities are the malformed offspring of sin.

"Although mainstream theology has largely bought into the dominant evolutionary narrative of 'Progress,'" writes philosopher John C. Clark, "the Bible's perspective on historical origins is quite contrary …. The 'primeval history' of Genesis 1–11, for example, portrays civilization as the 'fruit' not of human genius, but of alienation from the symbiotic lifeways of the 'Garden.' Its narrative of the 'Fall' is one of hard labor, murder, violence and predatory urbanism, culminating in the symbol of Babel's tower as the zenith of human rebellion against God and nature."[15]

The Post-Enlightenment lens of progress teaches us to see cities and civilization as a movement toward a better future. The Hebrew scriptures, however, give us images of cities that reflect "civilization-as-pathology," says Clark.

The ancient cities in the Hebrew scriptures were built

between 4000 and 2000 B.C.E., primarily in Egypt and Sumer (present-day Iraq). The texts tell the story of the first humans moving from pastoral nomadism to controlled agriculture to store cities or treasure cities, where wealth was kept and protected. With the development of agriculture, people broke the pattern of symbiotic lifeways. They settled. They narrowed their diet. With the development of store cities, people were severed from the process of raising their own food and providing for their own basic needs. This massive economic shift gave way to the development of serf and slave systems—and to armies to control and defend them. Cities are about mainly one thing: the flow of capital.

The altar as a center of violent sacrifice doesn't arrive on the biblical scene until the second human generation (Genesis 4) with the story of Cain and Abel. Here too the narrative reflects a deep tension between pastoral nomads and settled agriculturalists. Abel was "a keeper of sheep" and Cain a "tiller of the ground" (Genesis 4:2). "In the course of time," says the text, "Cain brought the Lord an offering of the first fruit of the ground, and Abel for his part brought the firstlings of his flock, their fat portions." Cain initiates the rite of sacrificing to God in order to ensure future harvest in this nascent experiment in agriculturalism. Here is an early example of humans choosing to go against the generative system set in place for them by God. In order to plant crops, one had to secure ground, and stabilize a community in one place to tend those crops. A community dependent on their own agricultural returns must begin storing seed and grain—and defending what they store, in other words, their excess.

The Genesis narrative continues, "And the Lord had regard for Abel and his offering, but for Cain and his offering the Lord had no regard" (Genesis 4:4-5). God indicates a clear preference for one economic system over another; God has regard for those who rely on God for their provisions.

Today urban life and rural, agricultural life are about as separate as they can be. It's hard to remember that the rise of agriculture and urbanization are intimately linked. It is not by chance that Cain murders Abel in a tilled field—his blood crying out from the plowed ground.

Cain's punishment is causal to his crime. Because he killed in a field, now the ground will not respond to his seeds. He will be forced to be a nomad—like Abel—but without the protection of a community, without the extravagant economy that held and sustained Abel. Torah scholar Avivah Zornberg says, "Cain's connection with the earth is disrupted. [Midrash commenter] Ramban emphasizes that restlessness is an inner quality of Cain's being, as essential character of his 'curse': 'His heart will not rest nor be quiet enough *to stand in one place.*'"[16]

"My punishment is greater than I can bear," says Cain to the Lord (Genesis 4:13). Afraid that now he will receive the same fate he just meted out to his brother, Cain pleads with God. And God marks him, "so that no one who came upon him would kill him" (Genesis 4:15).

The scripture continues, "Then Cain went away from the presence of the Lord, and settled in the land of Nod, east of Eden" (Genesis 4:16). Literally, he will "settle" in Nod, the land of "wandering." In the next verse, Cain was building a city and "he named the city Enoch, after his son" (Genesis 4:17).

"The city for Cain is . . . a material sign of his security," writes French theologian Jacques Ellul in *The Meaning of the City.* "He is responsible for himself and for his life. He is far from the Lord's face, and so he will shift for himself. The City is the direct consequence of his refusal to accept God's protection. Cain has built a City. For God's Eden he substitutes his own, for the goal given to his life by God, he substitutes a goal chosen by himself—just as he substituted his own security for God's."[17] Was Cain securing a stable environment for his son, Enoch, in reaction to the unstable world that Cain had been cast into?

"The City is called Enoch. 'Enoch' means 'initiation' or

'dedication,'" continues Ellul. "Cain dedicates a new world: 'Enoch' . . . Inauguration as opposed to Creation. Initiation, as opposed to the garden paradise. The city as opposed to Eden. It is certainly not unawares that Cain gave this name to his creation. Now he also is going to make the world over again. Cain is now going to reconstruct. In fact, the word should not be 'reconstruct,' but 'construct.' For in Cain's eyes it is not a beginning again, but a beginning. God's creation is seen as nothing." [18]

"By murder Cain has broken his relationship to humanity, to God and even the earth...," writes Detroit-based theologian Bill Wylie-Kellermann. "He has destroyed his home and so he sets out to build his own security. Cain's bold pretension is to construct his own new world. Violence is the kernel of alienation by which the brave new city is seeded." [19] In the descendents of Cain we find not only Jubal, father of "harp and pipe," but also Tubal-cain, forger of iron, brass, and maker of weapons. Cain is the progenitor of civilization: art and army.

"Cain ... reduces God to a hypothesis," says Ellul, "to the domain of the superfluous and the unreal. With Cain's beginning, with Enoch, we have a sure starting place for all of civilization. Paradise becomes a legend and creation a myth." Violence, according to the Bible, is at the heart of the urban civilizing project.

I am reading in a contemporary urban setting, in real time, these texts from the dawn of human history. What do they mean here and now? My "intepretive space" is the Columbia Heights neighborhood in the early years of the 21st century.

A few days after Donte was shot, his family asked friend Jacqueline Ponders to make their first public statement. "The family is praying that the person who is responsible for this crime, that God will convict their heart, that they will come forth and turn themselves in."[20] I hear the echoes of Cain and Abel, and of God who asks Cain, "Where is your brother?" This is the living scripture of the city.

•••

From Eden to the Fall, from Cain and Abel and the flood to Noah and the covenant, humanity cycles through participating in God's project and revolting against it. Genesis 6 shows the rise of the Nephilim (literally, "the fallen ones")—a race of violent giants who had "fallen" from the sky. They were a genetic mistake ("Those sons of the gods who cohabited with the daughters of Adam, and they bore children into them" Genesis 6:4)—the result of some primal human need to "re-engineer" the world in order to control and "improve" it, as theologian-activist

Ched Myers describes it. These were the "giants" who constructed the ancient cities with their towers and stair-cased pyramids or ziggurats.

God's response to this state of the world is to be sorry humans were ever made: "This race of men who I have created, I will wipe them off the face of the earth" (Genesis 6:6-7). And the waters began to rise. A tsunami-like flood cleaned the slate of all cities and slaves and armies; of all idolatry and false gods. In response to imperial homogenization, God restores divine diversity.

Genesis 10 jumps immediately into the post-Flood scenario, beginning with the "begats," telling us that unique populations and nations were returning. "These are the clans of Noah's sons [and, presumably, their wives], according to their lines of descent … From these, the nations spread out over the earth after the flood" (Genesis 10:32). The model from the Noah story is diversity. The earth is filled with a great variety of people, creatures, languages, arts, sciences, and social contracts.

Then the revolution against God begins again. In Genesis 11:1, the imperial project has returned: "Now the whole world had one language and a common speech." There is a jump into centralization and civilization. What do we know about "one language"? In the United States there is the English Only movement, which seeks to impose through legislation a sense of national unity. In France, there was a movement to remove "American expressions" from French vocabulary. "America is a threat to French glory," explained Raymond Rho in his article "Purity of the French Language," "because English is the language of diplomacy and business, the language of the victor. American military and economic power has translated into linguistic power." [21]

Languages are dying almost as quickly as the rain forest because of the imperial projects of the rich and powerful. Five hundred years ago in North America there were thousands of languages in diversified, decentralized cultures. Now there is one dominant language as a result of the U.S. colonial project. Monolingualism is one of the tools of imperialism. While a shared language may reduce conflict among neighboring cultures, an exclusive monolingualism is a tool of social control that too easily can be manipulated.

The building of the Tower (Genesis 11:1-9) is a Babylonian imperial project bent on consolidating power in an urban center, specifically through the use of Hebrew slaves. God's "divine counterstrategy" is to reconstruct diversity through the "confusion of languages" and the scattering of colonizers to all the ends of the earth.

"The nadir of the Fall," writes Myers in his article "The

Fall," "is thus narrated in the tale of the Tower of Babel. It symbolizes the archetypal project of urbanism, in which human, social, political, and economic power is concentrated rather than dispersed. The warning fable is a thinly veiled parody of Mesopotamian ziggurats, as [Evan] Eisenberg points out, in which the making of bricks (11:3) alludes to Israel's experience in slavery in Pharaoh's Egypt (Exodus 1). Such 'civilizational' projects are thus resolutely 'deconstructed' by the divine council [Genesis 11:7] in favor of the older vision of dispersed, tribal humanity living in diverse bio-regions (Genesis 11:5-9)." [22]

From the Babel story on, the walled city is regularly denounced in the Hebrew scriptures. In the oldest biblical stories the architecture of the city is seen as propaganda for an ethos of domination. Every ancient city had at its center an altar for making blood offerings, giving religious legitimization to the whole project of controlling others through military violence. While the human movement is toward centralization of power and capital, with its attendant militarization and slavery (the hallmarks of what it means to build an empire), God's movement is away from the city and toward the wilderness, where there is no permanent sacrificial altar and God lives nomadically in a tent. The biblical gesture of liberation is outward to the unknown and wild places, far from empire, far from imperial projects.

•••

Do the biblical anti-images of the city imbedded in the dominant Judeo-Christian worldview actually contribute to cities being places of poverty, injustice, racism? How do the biblical anti-images of the city relate to the motivation of Christians to "redeem", "help," "minister to," or "save" the sinful city? What are the assumptions, power dynamics, and social and economic locations involved?

"The biblical counternarrative of redemption from the Fall," Myers reminds us, recommences with Terah, father of Abraham, abandoning the Mesopotamian cities and, with his son, embracing "the new archetypal journey of liberation: following God's call back into the wilderness."

Every Passover begins with the famous line from Deuteronomy 26:5: "A wandering Aramean was my father …" Every Jew knows the saga by heart. For Jews, Christians, and Muslims it is the foundation of our liberation story. It also holds the complex historical shift in human culture from pastoral nomadism to civilization. The Passover narrative calls to mind the story of how stateless outlaws (*hapiru*) drift into Egypt, are held in slavery, and then are liberated into a promised land where they will eventually stop their nomadic ways and become a settled and domesticated people.

The Abraham narrative is located between two landmarks: The city of "Ur of the Chaldeans" (Genesis 11:28) and the "cave of Machpelah" (Genesis 23:9). The timestamp is about 2000 B.C.E. Terah (which means "takes them out") is the male leader of the tribe that moves from Ur. Terah's sons are Avram, Haran (whose son is Lot), and Nahor. His daughters are not mentioned. The most famous of his daughters-in-law is Sarai, wife of Avram. According to Robert A. Guisepi [23], most scholars today agree that Ur of the Chaldees was the Sumerian city of Ur. Today this city is called Tall al-Muqayyar (or Mughair) and is located near An Nasiriyah, a city on the currently highly militarized Baghdad-Basra highway in Iraq. Ur is one of the first cities to rise into the historical and archeological record and has imprinted itself into our language even today in the word "urban."

Urban design philosopher David Engwicht writes, "The connection between urban planning and religion may actually go back to the fifth millennium B.C.E. if one considers the evidence regarding Ur, the Babylonian port at the junction of the Euphrates and Tigris rivers," in his article "The Connection Between Urban Planning and Religion." [24]

In *Babylon is Everywhere*, Wolf Schneider takes the

reader through an imaginary tour of the ancient city. "A caravan arriving from the Arabian desert looks down from the last sandy hills into a flowering valley where a white city rises out of wheat fields and date palms. Its characteristic feature is a tiered pyramid, about a hundred feet high, built upon a black foundation, its terraces shimmering red, blue and gold," writes Schneider.[25] "A temple is erected on the uppermost platform, where priests pay homage to the moon god ... Arranged in a semi-circle around the imposing tower, in the midst of palm and cypress trees, are five temples and some treasury buildings with mighty walls, some almost three hundred feet long, with fountains and sacrificial altars in the inner courts ... Not far from the temples is the burial place of the kings ...."[26]

Religious beliefs formed the basis of all early city building, asserts Engwicht.[27] Priests were the technocrats who drove the planning process. Ancient cities were laid out according to celestial calculations so that the city design channeled the "supernatural energies" toward the center in order to reinforce the focus of religious and political power. With all this in mind, how might I read the religious message in the lay-out of Washington, D.C.? And how might you read the religious message of the architecture around you?

Chapter 2
With the Tongues of Empires

If I speak in the tongues of mortals and of angels, but have not love, I am a noisy gong or a clanging cymbal.
—1 Corinthians 13:1

Architecturally, Washington, D.C., is a classical city built along the same theo-urban lines as the ancient Middle Eastern cities. In 1791, African-American architect and astronomer Benjamin Banneker—one of the few free Blacks living in the area—surveyed, along with Andrew Ellicott, the ten-mile square of the Federal Territory in preparation for the new capital.[28] D.C.'s boundaries were based on Banneker's celestial calculations. (Banneker, a scientific genius, exchanged letters with Thomas Jefferson on the abolishment of slavery and the establishment of an Office of Peace.) At the request of George Washington, Frenchman Pierre L'Enfant arrived in what would be Washington, D.C., in March of 1791 to begin his preliminary design for urban planning based on Banneker's measurements. The work would be like "turning a savage wilderness into a garden of Eden," wrote L'Enfant to Washington. [29]

Initially D.C. was not built with defensive positions. When the Civil War began, only Fort Washington, built to guard against enemy ships coming up the Potomac River, existed to defend the city. After the Union defeat at Manassas the Army Corps of Engineers built a defense system to ring the city consisting of 68 forts and 93 batteries with 807 cannons and 98 mortars in place. Twenty miles of rifle trenches flanked the bristling strongholds, joined by more than 30 miles of military roads over which companies of soldiers and guns could move. By 1865, Washington D.C. was one of the most heavily fortified cities in the world. [30]

Now the Civil War bunkers are only tourist stops, but Washington, D.C., is still a "fortified city." The real "fortification" grid is a 30 nautical mile lopsided ring of restricted airspace around the D.C. region known as the Air Defense Identification Zone. Within that ring is a 13-15 nautical mile strict no-fly zone known as the Flight Restricted Zone that protects the White House and Capitol Hill. An invisible wall surrounds the city, built with the interlaced views of security cameras on the exterior of all federal buildings and on most major street intersections, a U.S. Army blimp with electro-optical/infrared cameras that provides "real time images and other forms of intelligence to ground commanders,"[31] F-16 jets from Andrews Air Force base that regularly fly a grid over the city, the Black Hawk helicopters that provide 24/7 coverage, and the mobile surface-to-air missile units that patrol the downtown areas or park at highway entrances.

All of this is part of the District's "layered" post-Sept. 11 militarized defense system. For the most part, all these layers serve to protect the White House, Capitol, World Bank, and a few other high-profile targets clustered in the city center. If they protect the poor and working-class neighborhoods of Washington, D.C., it is an incidental benefit. More often, they serve to add a layer of militarization to the existing layer of social violence.

•••

How do "security issues" in the inner city, especially in post-Sept. 11 Washington, D.C., help us understand in a new way Jesus' metaphor of "a house divided" (Matthew 12:25)? How do we read the Apostle Paul's discussion of the "dividing wall" in Ephesians 2 in light of current security threats?

Paul writes: "For Christ Jesus is our peace, who has made us both one, and has broken down the dividing wall of hostility by abolishing in his flesh the law of commandments and ordinances, that he might create in himself one new human in place of the two, so making peace, and might reconcile us both to God in one body through the cross, thereby bringing the hostility to an end" (Ephesians 2:14-16).

The Greek phrase "dividing wall" can also be translated as "security fence" or "security wall." The symmetric literary structure of Ephesians 2:14-16 makes parallel the idea of "breaking down the dividing wall" and "making powerless the law." The traditional interpretation reads this as a metaphorical division between Jews and non-Jews, with "the law" referring directly to the Mosaic law. But reading Paul's comments in the post-Sept. 11 context raises questions about the extent to which laws can provide us with security and whether heightening divisions between people is fundamentally anti-Christian.

In Washington, D.C., the stratification isn't only physical, it's also economic. The White House and Capitol are 2.5 miles and 3.3 miles, respectively, from my house in Columbia Heights. The fiscal year 2006 federal budget illustrates a pattern of priorities that has only continued to stratify since then. In April 2005, the U.S. Congress "passed a $2.6 trillion budget resolution for fiscal 2006 after the House reached a deal with Senate negotiators to shave $10 billion from Medicaid," reported the *Washington Times*.[32] "The budget virtually freezes domestic spending at $391 billion, with $33 billion going to homeland security, and will hold military spending to $420 billion." In reality, there was no holding back military spending. A week after this budget was passed President Bush requested another $72.4 billion for war-related expenses, which brought spending on just the Iraq War in FY2006 to $100 billion.[33] Funding for social programs—such as adult learning programs, Section 8 housing, and student loans—dropped.

The people in my neighborhood know exactly what those numbers and decisions mean—and how it will affect them. At 33 percent, D.C. has a higher child poverty rate than any of the states, according to the National Center for Children in Poverty.[34] Fifty-six percent of births in D.C. were "out of wedlock" in 2004.[35] D.C.'s overall poverty rate is 19.6 percent. It ranks at the bottom of the national average— one notch above rural Mississippi.[36] The life expectancy of an African-American man in D.C. is 58, compared with American men in general, which is 73. Half of the District's population of young black men is "under criminal justice supervision."[37] The other half just live here.

In the early 1990s, the U.S. Census Bureau put out interesting data about poverty rates in the District. And, while most residents may not spend time in the data sets, they do know the percentages in their bones. Out of the dozens of census tracts that make up the larger Washington, D.C.-metropolitan area, 36 of them had poverty rates greater than 30 percent—and all of those were located within the District.

"Despite the Washington region's overall prosperity, the number of high-poverty tracts rose during the 1990s, their population increased, and their poverty deepened," according to *Housing in the Nation's Capital* (2003), a report by the Fannie Mae Foundation. "The total number of high-poverty census tracts in the Washington region increased from 36 in 1990 to 43 in 2000. The number of extreme-poverty tracts (with poverty rates greater than 40 percent) rose even more dramatically—from 10 to 23," the report concluded.[38] In part the data uncovers the growing gap between neighbors or those who ride the subway together. While the language of prosperity is trumpeted in some corners of the city, whole neighborhoods understand that the music of success is not meant for them.

•••

The strong anti-city images found in the earliest biblical texts continue to shape and form our symbols and mythology as Christians today. These negative biblical images have had a huge impact on the "urban planning" movement of the last 200 years. The city was seen as the center of evil, particularly a location of sexual deviance and sin.

The Judeo-Christian gaze of many urban reformers and architects influenced what they saw and didn't see and how they interpreted it. Sociologist Elizabeth Wilson, in *The Sphinx in the City: Urban Life, the Control of Disorder, and Women*, argues that "the 'urban consciousness' that developed during the 19th and early 20th century, was essentially a 'male consciousness' which was preoccupied with a 'sexual unease' brought on by the increased possibility of sexual encounters outside the constraints of family which is inherent in the city." [39] In reality, this sometimes means that cities are laid out in ways that reflect men's urban priorities rather than women's. Tracking the validity of this claim and documenting its effects has led to a new exploration of the "gendered realities" of urban life.

In Washington, D.C.'s high-poverty neighborhoods, women substantially outnumber men—and make up a large share of single-parent households. "Specifically," concluded Fannie Mae's *Housing in the Nation's Capital* report, "for every 10 women living in high-poverty neighborhoods in 2000 there were only 7.7 men, compared with nine men for every 10 women in the city as a whole."[40] Poor neighborhoods are often populated primarily by women who exist in an urban architecture designed against them.

After 20 years of living in Columbia Heights, I am also

seeing a new shift. One that continues to show how the tides of capital ebb and flow through urban neighborhoods. An example of this new shift was the opening of a subway stop in Columbia Heights in 1999. With the Metro came the popping up of high-rise condos built over the top of what had been several community gardens where neighbors gathered each summer to trade excess squash and tomatoes while carrying buckets of water from a nearby apartment building. The census data now describes Columbia Heights as a neighborhood in the process of shifting from an extreme-poverty census tract to merely a high-poverty census tract. As of 2000, 22 percent of the Columbia Heights population was under 18. The poverty rate was 26 percent. Eleven percent of the housing was public or subsidized. Also 33 percent of the population was foreign born and 55 percent of the population had moved in the last five years.[41] The neighborhood is moving from a poor, unemployed or under-employed, multi-generational African-American community of mostly non-homeowners to something quite different.

The shift that is happening is called gentrification. High-income individuals are moving in. Often, for a very cheap price, wealthier folks buy houses that have fallen into disrepair, either because the tenants couldn't afford to keep them up or the landlords refused to do so. They rehab the house and either live in it or to sell it at a substantial profit (also known as "flipping"). Occasionally the houses they buy are abandoned, but more often the purchasing process displaces families who have lived in the neighborhood for years, sometimes generations, but who were never able to own their own home.

For several years I lived next door to the Thomas family. During that period their household consisted of Hazel, who worked as an apartment manager; her husband Marshall, a shipping clerk at Andrews Air Force base; their adult son Reggie, who worked for a company renovating kitchens; and Hazel and Marshall's teen-age grandson. Reggie's parents had moved into that house by 1960.[42]

After Hazel and Marshall died, Reggie couldn't keep the house going on his own. He was living in only two rooms. The rest of the house had been abandoned to the failed plumbing, electrical, and heating systems. The water and sewer company put a lien on it. The mortgage company foreclosed and sold the house to a real estate developer for $190,000. The developer then sold it to a married couple for $360,000 who, within three years, had "flipped" it for a *profit* of $500,000.[43]

What does scripture say about such dealings? It's not that Reggie necessarily wanted to stay in the house where he grew up. But, then again, he ultimately had no choice.

He didn't receive just compensation for the more than 40 years his family had lived there and contributed to the life of the neighborhood. Yet a couple with enough assets to own more than one property could live there for less than three years and extract $500,000 out of the property. Did they do anything "wrong"? Not according to the law. In fact, they made a strategically advantageous financial move. The biblical prophet Isaiah, however, thinks differently. "Woe to those who join house to house, who add field to field, till there is no place where the poor may dwell alone in the midst of the land!" (Isaiah 5:8).

•••

Though the police had no leads in Donte Manning's murder, they thought it was probably an act of retaliation against the residents of the Warner Apartments on 13th Street. Neighbor Larry Bellinger told me, "My initial thoughts were that the shooting was related to what I saw when I got home from work that evening. I was walking toward my house from the direction of Euclid Street and looked across the street to see the police bringing several people out of the Warner in handcuffs. Turned out to be a drug raid in process." The police arrested three people. The shooting was one of at least three within about 20 minutes in the northwest section of the District—in addition to Donte, two other men were shot and another killed.[44]

Following a series of violent incidents in 1995, members of the Christian Peacemaker Teams (CPT) worked with the Warner Apartment residents in an urban peacemaking project. CPT was conceived in 1984 to train Christian pacifists in the same discipline and self-sacrifice that soldiers devote to war. It has teams putting themselves in harm's way in Iraq, Colombia, Israel-Palestine border, the U.S.-Mexican border, and in the U.S. and Canada in places of heightened violence. In 1995, CPT's bright yellow flyers were passed out to everyone living in the Warner Apartment building and to nearby residents. They announced volunteers would be stopping by to ask questions of tenants and neighbors about problems in the neighborhood and possible solutions. The "listening project" format hoped to identify "transformative rather than imposed solution to the mutual crisis of violence in our community."

The CPT project did reduce violence and increase safety over time. There were "orange hat" neighborhood patrols to keep watch over kids outside and limit the scope of the open-air drug market, communication with the police improved, and "beat cops" returned. There were after-school and summer projects for kids and some local teens were connected with job services. However, the neighborhood population continued to turn over—people moving every three to five years, primarily for economic reasons—so lack of stability undermined long-term organizing. CPT moved on to other projects. Ten years later the drug dealing was worse than in 1995.

On that spring night in March 2005, the drug dealers flipped the script on the cops and came back guns ablazing. The result? Donte Manning lying in a pool of blood on the sidewalk outside his apartment.

•••

The District's drug economy centers around crack cocaine and marijuana, with heroin and crystal meth on the increase. Almost all the crack and marijuana comes from Central and South America through Miami and then, along with guns, up Interstate 95 to New York City, with drop-offs in D.C., Baltimore, and Philadelphia.

Approximately 75 percent of the coca cultivated for processing into cocaine is currently grown in Colombia, and Colombian drug trafficking organizations are responsible for most of the cocaine production, transportation, and distribution.

In March 2001, I was in Colombia with a faith-based

peace team, Witness for Peace. Our mission was to get a firsthand look at the supply side of the "war on drugs" and see for ourselves the on-the-ground effects of "Plan Colombia," the $1.3 billion U.S. military aid package Congress had approved in the fall of 2000. We met with a wide range of people, from local pastors and human rights workers to U.S. Embassy and Colombian government officials. In Puerto Asis, Putumayo, in southern Colombia, we also met with indigenous leaders from around the region. One man explained the role of the coca plant (which is the organic base for cocaine) in his culture:

> Coca is a spiritual and medicinal plant for many native people. It is the plant that brought life in some of our stories. We never thought of it as an "evil plant." It is part of our life, our family, our story. It is part of who we are. The Murai people have always used coca to try to heal the world. We don't think eradication should happen on the Murai lands. It is when coca is processed into something else and produces wealth, and then those who want to have power over that wealth…that is when conflict and violence and death come with coca.

We also met with representatives of rural farmers' organizations, who showed us the other end of the cocaine production process—the coca cash crop. It was a scary trip to the farm of this subsistence farming family. Jostling over unpaved jungle back roads deep into guerilla-controlled territory, we had to move quickly in order to be back to the town of Puerto Asis before sunset. The farmer accompanied us and explained his local economics.

"Most farms are about nine and a half hectares or less," he told me. "Half a hectare is beans, and half a hectare is corn, then two hectares of yucca, two of plantains, two left fallow, and 2.5 in coca. Three kilos of coca leaves can be collected per hectare per harvest. It takes 12.5 kilos to make one aroba of unprocessed coca leaves. One aroba is processed to produce 18 grams of coca paste."

His farm, worked cooperatively with several other families, was definitely a commercial operation. It was clean and well-kept. The processing shed for converting coca leaves to coca paste was rustic. It looked like a tobacco drying barn.

Coca leaves are run through a shredder, then spread out on the floor. Salt or cement is sprinkled on them and then mixed to advance the drying process until the leaves turn black or "burned." Then the leaves are placed in a 50-gallon drum of gasoline and Triple 15 fertilizer is added to extract the active ingredients from the leaves. After the coca soup sits for a few days, the liquid is separated from the leaves and the leaves are recycled for fertilizer. Sodium bicarbonate is added to the liquid to create a coagulate. Then the liquid, now mostly gasoline, is drained off. What's left is a thick sticky green paste that contains the chloral hydrate—the active ingredient in cocaine. This paste is what is sold to the narcotraffickers. The transformation from paste into powder or crystal cocaine is very expensive and is done at sophisticated laboratories deep in the jungle. Small farmers have nothing to do with this end of things.

According to our host farmer's estimates, most of the small farm owners in the Putamayo region of southern Colombia make about 300,000 pesos per month per hectare of coca—about $US100-200. Minimum wage for a family of 4 in Colombia was about 1,000,000 pesos per month. In other words, the average small farmer with 2-3 hectares of coca makes just enough money from coca to bring his or her income to half or a little more of the federal minimum wage. The coca crop provides cash to buy clothes, sugar, and pay for school for the children—that's all.

We also met with the mayor of Puerto Asis, Manuel Alzate. His armed guards kept a sharp watch at the entrance—their 9mm Uzis at the ready. Mayor Alzate was a former diocesan Catholic priest who studied in France and served in Cali, Colombia. He wrote two books on the history of the Catholic Church in Colombia, but his liberal views got him excommunicated in the 1960s. In 1973, he came to Puerto Asis where he bought a small farm. "This now is my life of service," he told me. "I am a public servant." A week earlier he had been attacked. Someone had thrown a stick of dynamite at him.

"Before coca, Puerto Asis was at peace," said Mayor Alzate. "We produced our crops and lived in peace. Then coca came in. Then money came in. Then violence came in. Then guerillas. Then the drug lords, 'The Macetos,' which are now the paramilitaries. Now death touches everyone. Sunday a young man died. Yesterday two more bodies were found."

According to Alzate, the local farmers make approximately $US200 when they sell a kilo of coca paste to the narcotraffickers. "In New York, a kilo of street coke sells for approximately $150,000," he told us. That price holds true for Washington, D.C. "It is not fair that we continue to die and pile up dead bodies here while all the money [from drugs] stays in the United States and you don't take up your part of the responsibility," continued Alzate. "You must stop the demand. Only then will it be just."

In Puerto Asis, I also met with Fr. Alfonso, a Franciscan

priest, who received regular death threats from the army, paramilitary, and guerilla groups for his work in the community. He described to me the situation:

> There is a very deep faith among the poor people here. It is very passionate, very hopeful, the people feel God all around them. We are a believing people but we are also poor and have been beaten down. Our people have been completely forgotten by the central state.
>
> The people used to produce bananas but it began to cost more to transport them than they could be sold for. Then coca entered this area. Now the campesinos live off of coca. Then the [aerial] fumigation comes and they don't only fumigate coca but also all the food. After coca, then comes the guerilla. Fumigation has happened here for years. Then when the farmers strike against it, the state finally responds with huge militarization of the region. The 24th Brigade comes in here. Then the paramilitaries come in here. This is a story filled with many deaths.
>
> Of the 207 funerals performed in

this church last year, 97 of them were assassinations. But we cannot speak openly about this. If you speak out you will get a visit. So the law of this region is silence.

People come to me and say 'Father, help me. The [Army, paramilitaries, or guerrillas] have stolen my child.' So I get on the motorcycle and ride to the military camp and demand the child back. The hardest thing is when I can't go and I have to tell the parents that they will have to go themselves.

The effects of this "Colombia-to-Columbia Heights" connection can be seen every day in Donte Manning's neighborhood in the form of discarded crack bags, late-night weapons fire, and prostitution.

Here again I was hearing stories about the altars that greed built and the human sacrifices these cults require—especially the blood of children, the most vulnerable.

•••

In 2002, some 352 metric tons of export-quality cocaine was available in U.S. markets. Of the cocaine that enters the United States, 72 percent passed through the

Mexico/Central America corridor. Another 27 percent moved through the Caribbean and 1 percent comes directly from South America.[45] The three dealers arrested in the Warner Apartments on the evening Donte Manning was shot were probably part of a loose confederation of neighborhood men in their twenties who sell and use crack and marijuana.

In most cities today the global drug economy mirrors the "legal" global trade network. It is the shadow empire that runs beneath the trade policies, military ventures, and political alliances of the American Empire run from the White House, twenty blocks south of Columbia Heights.

Historically, coca leaves were used less as a stimulant and more as a means to suppress hunger pangs. Coca was especially used by indigenous communities who were forced into slave labor by the Conquistadors. In other words, it was used to help an oppressed people survive the dehumanizing pressures of the Spanish Empire.

What are the hungers that people use crack to suppress? As Christians, how might we address the hunger of the crack-addicted? How do we contribute to their oppression? What are the demons that feed off addiction? How do we restore the demon-infested to health? How do the demons brought on by addiction critique the health of our community and society?

In Mark, Jesus links dealing with demons as a precursor to overthrowing the present reign - you must bind the strong man before you can plunder his house (Mark 3:27). "Mark's concern is not only liberation from the specific structures of oppression embedded in the dominant social order of Roman Palestine," writes activist and theologian Ched Myers in *Binding the Strong Man*, "it also includes the spirit and practice of domination ultimately embedded in the human personality and corporately in human history as a whole. The struggle against the powers and the individual and collective will to dominate is articulated over and over again in different ways throughout the story."[46] The drug economy, the crack house, the stashes kept in loose bricks around the neighborhood, the women who trade their bodies for a rock of crack in the abandoned building two blocks from my house—all these teach me about demons, and empire, and where Jesus walks and heals and liberates.

Chapter 3
All Roads Lead to Starbucks

Swerve me? Ye cannot swerve me. ...The path to my fixed purpose
is laid with iron rails, whereon my soul is grooved to run.
—Captain Ahab, *Moby Dick* [47]

Teenage organizers in my neighborhood say these demons flourish in a "culture of neglect." These youth sponsored a presentation called "A Reality Tour of Youth Violence in D.C." They addressed the issues of family, violence, and communities abandoned by the society at large. The Youth Action Research Group (YARG) interviewed black and Latino youth all over D.C. to get their perspectives on youth violence and youth-based solutions. In 2004, 24 of the District's 198 homicide victims were 17 years old or younger. At least 22 of those youth died as a result of gun violence, reported YARG. Four of them were killed in gang-related violence within blocks of the YARG office in Columbia Heights.

"[S]ome people are in a gang because it is like a family for them," one teenager reported to 16-year-old YARG researcher Denisse. "They don't have no family, they don't have no support—so they get that support from the street... and they join a gang. Just because you're in a gang, you shouldn't just get locked up—they just need help. They need love." [48]

Similar to the reform movement of the Desert Fathers and Mothers who left the cities in order to resist the domestication of Christianity and to minister to those on the margins, there is a similar call for Christians to engage the areas of cities that are coated in neglect. "The call for Christians," writes Margaret McKenna in *Schools for Conversion*, "is to relocate to the abandoned places of Empire." [49] It doesn't mean these places are unaffected by empire—quite the opposite—however, they are not useful to the economic engine of empire (except to provide cannon fodder in wars to protect economic interests).

The youth involved in YARG make the connection between the "war on terrorism" and the war on them. On a community e-mail list discussing gangs, the YARG members note that one respondent posted, "I've already posted the solution [to gangs]. Treat gang members and suspected gang members as terrorists and gang activity as terrorism. Label them terrorists and they won't be on the street. They'll be held down in Git'mo. If they are labeled as terrorists we could get federal funds and federal agents to get in here and get them out of our neighborhoods." Another neighbor added, "The police have my blessing to kill them off one by one."

In 2005, Donte Manning was the fifth juvenile to be murdered in the District. Two were victims of child abuse. The others, a 17-year-old and 16-year-old, were shot while in cars in Southeast Washington.[50]

These organizers at YARG are keenly aware of the gentrification issue, which they see as a root cause of violence. "It's hard to see your apartment building closed," said LeKeisha at a neighborhood gathering hosted by YARG, "for a Starbucks to move in."

As a poet, I'm not looking for linear progressions, but rather images or icons to interpret the world around me. I ask what the image means in the local culture. What are its cultural and historical resonances? Where does it take me if I start following it? LeKeisha alerts me to Starbucks. She identifies it with imperial power because, from her perspective, she and her family were forced from their home—made economic refugees—by a coffee corporation that serves rich people.

•••

According to legend, Starbucks, which started in Seattle in 1971, is named after the first mate in Melville's novel *Moby Dick*. Starbuck is the most overtly "Christian" of the characters in this great biblical morality tale of modern man against God. He believes that Christianity offers a way to interpret the world around him. He provides a moderate, cautious, counter-perspective to Ahab's mania. Starbuck quotes Malachi 4:2 to Ahab, reminding him about the "rising of the sun of righteousness with healing in its wings," but says calling to the Lord at midnight is in vain.

When the casks of precious whale oil collected by the crew of the Pequod begin leaking, Starbuck appeals to Ahab's concern for his investors. Ahab is focused on the white whale and says, "Let it leak." "What will the owners say, sir?" Starbuck asks. "Owners, owners?" fires back Ahab, "Thou art always prating to me, Starbuck, about those miserly owners, as if the owners were my conscience. But look ye, the only real owner of anything is its commander; and hark ye, my conscience is in this ship's keel!"

Ahab grabs a loaded musket and aims it towards Starbuck. "There is one God that is Lord over the earth," exclaims Ahab, "and one Captain that is lord over the Pequod." [51]

Starbucks, the restaurant coffee king, shows the benevolent face of empire. "You get more than the finest coffee when you visit a Starbucks—you get great people, first-rate music and a comfortable and upbeat meeting place," says Starbucks CEO Howard Schultz. "Starbucks is rekindling America's love affair with coffee, bringing romance and fresh flavor back to the brew."[52] It allows workers to buy shares in the company. It provides health and education benefits for part-timers and domestic partners. It supports socially responsible corporate practices. One could say that Starbucks—as long as it's making money—provides a moderating voice in the world of global business. Yet, like their namesake, they do not lead a prophetic mutiny against unfettered global capitalism that crushes the poor, nor are they able to prevent a grandmother being forced from her apartment to make room for their newest "upbeat meeting place."

Of its roughly 80,000 "partners," most of them are twenty-somethings [53] in what they call "JoeJobs"—barristas serving coffee or "joe" as it was called in the Navy during World War I. Since most of the available jobs in the United States are in the service sector, Starbucks is molding and training America's youth into the service economy that is their future.

The coffee economy, of course, extends worldwide. Starbucks buys its fine arabica beans from Central America, Africa, and Indonesia. According to the *International Herald Tribune*, the coffee crisis in 2001 "cost some 260,000 farmers in Costa Rica, El Salvador and Nicaragua their jobs, pushing many families to near-starvation. The U.S. Agency for International Development estimates that because of the glut, 600,000 growers in Central America found themselves without work."[54] People who were dependent on the coffee harvest were forced to migrate to the cities or to try to emigrate to the United States—often entering illegally. Coffee is the second most extensively traded commodity after oil. The United States is by far the world's biggest coffee importer, trailed by Germany, Italy, and Japan.

One can follow the aroma of Starbucks into unusual places. These days a local neighborhood almost always has tentacles pressing on it from the global economy. And the global economy, in its current imperial manifestation, is almost always protected and maintained by violence. This was the nature of Rome when it extended its reach to Palestine and it is the nature of American Empire too.

•••

In Washington, D.C., it is easy to see the connections because everything is proximate. The powerful White House is two and a half miles from the poverty of Columbia Heights. World Bank headquarters are only a few miles from D.C.'s failing reservoir and lead-filled water supply from a deteriorating sewer system. Homeless people live beneath the overpass that leads to the Pentagon. And CIA headquarters are tucked back into the pastoral, verdant landscape of Langley, Virginia, about ten miles from Columbia Heights.

Gary Schroen is former CIA station chief in Pakistan and author of *First In: An Insider's Account of How the CIA Spearheaded the War on Terror in Afghanistan.* According to an interview I heard with Schroen on National Public Radio,[55] he was called out of retirement two days after the terrorist attacks of September 11, 2001. His bosses handed him a new mission targeting Osama bin Laden.

"Your basic marching order are to … capture bin Laden, kill him, and bring his head back in a box on dry ice … ," Cofer Black, chief of CIA counterterrorist center, told Schroen. As for other al Qaeda leaders, Cofer ordered "I want their heads up on pikes." "Sir, those are the clearest orders I've ever received," replied Schroen. "I can certainly make pikes out in the field but I don't know what I'll do about dry ice to bring the head back but we'll manage something."

Schroen, his six-man team, and three pilots were the only U.S. government personnel on the ground in Afghanistan between September 26 and October 19, 2001. Over the next few weeks, Schroen paid $5 million in bribes to Afghan commanders, paved the way for U.S. military forces to enter the country, and armed anti-al Qaeda fighters with silencer-equipped machine guns and grenades.

As the days and weeks passed, supplies ran low. Schroen recalls drafting a re-supply request that listed more money and other items. "Somebody put in 100 pounds of Starbucks coffee and two little percolators … ," said Schroen. "We thought nobody's going to send us that. And sure enough when the helicopter arrived there was a hundred pounds of Starbucks coffee. We were just ecstatic. We dropped everything else. We even had ten million dollars sitting there and we said 'Put that stuff in the corner … Let's make coffee.'"

The NPR reporter said in the story, "Fortified with mocha java, Gary Schroen began working to orient U.S. army special forces … and to hire a small group of local assassins."

The $3 many Americans pay for a Starbucks latte is equivalent to the daily wage of a Central American coffee picker.[56] On the night Donte Manning was shot I was preparing for a trip to El Salvador to attend the 25th anniversary of the assassination of Archbishop Oscar Romero, known as the Saint of the Americas. In El Salvador, nearly 12 percent of the nation's arable land is planted in coffee. In 2004 coffee represented 2.5 percent of El Salvador's Gross National Product and 19.8 percent of the agricultural product. Forty-seven percent of El Salvador's coffee is shipped to the United States.[57] In 2001, remittances back to El Salvador from Salvadorans in the United States amounted to 14 percent of El Salvador's GDP.[58] So much U.S. currency was flowing into El Salvador that in 2001 the country "dollarized"—ended use of *colones* and adopted the U.S. dollar as its national currency. Approximately 20 percent—one in five—Salvadorans live in the United States. In the D.C. neighborhoods of Columbia Heights, Mount Pleasant, and Cardozo/Shaw, Hispanics make up 21 percent of the population, while the District's overall population is approximately 7 percent Latino.[59]

One of the Youth Action Research Group activists from my neighborhood, Denisse, said, "No one ever bothers to ask for the youth's input on violence. We care because we are the ones getting shot every day .... It hurts to watch the news hoping and praying we don't see someone we know. We don't like seeing our same friends who were supposed to graduate with us behind bars."

The biblical book Lamentations says when children and youth are weak and discouraged it is from the failure of Israel to keep God's covenant. According to the text, the prophet Jeremiah came out of retirement to sit in a cave near Jerusalem's gate and sing funeral dirges for the city—for her women and her children. Tears run down his face. "My children are desolate," he says (Lamentations 1:16). "Lift up your hands toward the Lord for the life of the young children that faint for hunger in the top of every street" (2:19). And, most poignantly, "The children ask for bread, and no one breaks it for them" (4:4).

I hear the voices of the YARG youth when I read these passages. "Discouragement destroys my spirit little by little," said Denisse. "When other people don't believe in you," said 16-year-old Sukeria, "then you feel like you are not worth anything at all." YARG member Maria (aka Ghost) shared a poem she wrote for YARG founder Natalie Avery. "She showed me a new place within my barrio where youth could fight for their beliefs by creating a space for my world, enlightening a change."

Families are very fragile. Often they can't take the pressure we, as a society, put on them. Children and teenagers are not terrorists. They learn what we teach them.

In the passage from Lamentations, the image of bread reappears. Here is another kind of altar on which bread is given or withheld. In what ways may we listen for, recognize, and tell the gospel story in this kind of city space, where an imperial economy and security forces are surrounded by poor neighborhoods like mine?

This question involves both discernment and proclamation. It asks about the disciplines of prayer and urban contemplation by which Christians enter into and intercede for the city. It engages the practice of biblical interpretation or hermeneutics to read urban architecture (physical, social, and spiritual). It moves toward an examination of the diverse forms in which the good news may be narrated, visualized, and embodied.

•••

In the gospels, especially in Mark because of its literary structure, I can feel the rhythms that flow between the wilderness and the city. The wilderness edges are where the Jesus Movement is at home, comfortable, grounded. The city center is where the Temple is the architectural and symbolic culmination of the civilizing project. Urban design philosopher David Engwicht writes, "The significance of much of the imposition of order on city form was primarily an act of defining identity and creation of a sense of certainty about that identity."[60]

There is a constant tension between the symbols of the centralizing power of the Davidic dynasty and its scribal implementers, the religious authorities, and the symbols of the decentralized power of the kinship model promoted by Jesus in the wilderness or in small towns or on the margins of the city. He only goes to the city center in order to harshly critique the symbols of power—both religious and political—and interpret them in new ways (which are really old ways) for the disciples.

The gospels have a variety of city images. When the devil tempts Jesus by taking him to the pinnacle of the Temple, Matthew's gospel implies the devil controls the Temple and the city surrounding it (Matthew 4:5). In the parable of the king giving a wedding feast for his son, the murderous wedding guests are all from the city and the king retaliates by "burning up their city" and sends his servants to the "highways," the marginal areas between the city and the country, to find more suitable invitees (Matthew 22:7). During Jesus' meal at the house of a Pharisee, the woman who anoints Jesus' feet with oil is called a "woman of the city, a sinner" (Luke 7:37). In Matthew 12, Jesus begins hinting to the Pharisees that there is one in their presence now who is "greater than the temple"—greater than the religious-political power of the city. In Mark 13, Jesus tries to leave the Temple space after a sharp critique of the misuse of religious tithing laws that made priests rich but pushed the poor into destitution. But his disciples seem put off by his incisive judgment and appear to want him to soften his rhetoric by praising the wonderful architecture of the Temple. They call him back for a discussion on the symbolic power of architecture. ("Look, Teacher, what wonderful stones and what wonderful buildings!") He interprets the Temple for them, very plainly: "Do you see these great buildings? There shall not be left here one stone upon another that shall not be thrown down" (Mark 13:2).

In Luke's gospel there are some qualified positive associations with the Temple. The temple priest Zechariah received a vision about the birth of his son John the Baptist (though Zechariah must enter a wilderness of silence following the vision), and the prophet Anna embodied what was righteous and good about God's covenant with the Jews and lived it out in the Temple space.

•••

In Washington, D.C., I can walk downtown around the White House and Capitol to study the symbolic power of architecture. But, if I want to read scripture from the margins, I stand in Columbia Heights. Sometimes it feels like I'm walking in the living narrative of the gospels, a time-warped virtual reality. When I want to see live gospel stories, I go to the Amoco gas station at 14th and Euclid Streets NW.

One Saturday morning I stopped at the gas station for a cup of coffee. I was standing at the front door lowering my lips to a steaming Styrofoam cup when the Wonder Bread truck pulled up to unload the weekend deliveries. The driver opened the cargo bay doors and began off-loading flats of bread. Across the parking lot, a woman in her late 40s saw the truck full of bread and made directly for it. She was thin. Her clothes were not clean. Her face was drawn with cold.

The driver seemed nervous to leave her standing next to his open bay doors while he wheeled the deliveries into the store. He glanced at me as if to say, "Keep an eye on things." She did indeed appear to be weighing whether she could grab a couple of loaves and run. She didn't. When the driver returned, she asked him very politely, but with a certain level of desperation, if she could have some bread. "Sister," he said, "it's not mine to give." She asked again, for just one loaf. With some anguish, he turned his back on her, saying again, "It's not mine to give." She walked away.

The driver looked at me, embarrassed. He seemed genuinely ashamed that he didn't give bread to a sister in need. The driver was correct in saying that the bread was not his to give. There are inventories to be filled and every item must be accounted for, lest he be accused of stealing. In one sense, the bread is "owned" by the Wonder Bread parent company, Interstate Bakeries Corp. In another sense—a more human sense—bread is to be shared.

In the crisp morning air, Jesus' question in Luke's gospel was stretched like a spiritual high-tension wire between the delivery driver and myself—Who among you, when your child asks for bread, would give a stone? (Luke 11:11).

And where do the gleaning rights of the poor (detailed in Leviticus 19 and 23) fit in our modern economy?

How does the architecture of Washington, D.C., define the spirit of the people who live here (see Mark 13:1-3)? Where is the narrative space of a city? Whose narrative? How do we tell the gospel story in the city space?

•••

One autumn, another scene unfolded at that same intersection. I attended an impromptu prayer service on the sidewalk across from the gas station. A young man, Erlin, had been killed two nights earlier at that location in a gang altercation. The word went through the neighborhood that his mother wanted to pray.

Twenty people were crowded around a scrawny Department of Public Works-issue maple tree. Someone used masking tape to fix Erlin's picture to the tree trunk. His elementary-school-age nieces and nephews held votive candles purchased at the Dollar Store. Erlin's buddies from his "crew" were there too. They lined up behind his mother, forming a kind of honor guard. They all wore dark glasses; a few had guns shoved down the front of their nylon running pants. Some, out of respect for his mother, had put their weapons—thick chains and baseball bats with nails hammered into the ends—behind the dumpster a few yards away.

A woman from Erlin's church led prayers. The little kids said they hoped "Uncle Erlin" was in heaven. Local activists pleaded for an end to the violence, begging his crew not to retaliate.

Finally, his mother asked to speak.

In her soft Jamaican accent, she said how much she loved her son. She said he struggled to do the right thing, and that watching him struggle had broken her heart. Then she turned to his friends—his fellow gang members—and said the most amazing thing. "He was my son," she said. "You were his brothers. Now you are my sons and I am your mother. Now we are family. This is the way it is." She expected his "brothers" to be at her table for jerk chicken and potatoes any time they were hungry. She expected them to help her fix things around the apartment. They must come to her with their problems, and she would pray for each of them every day.

In the gathering dark, I heard the line from John's gospel echo and twist. "When Jesus saw his mother and the disciple whom he loved standing by, he said, 'Woman, behold your son!' Then he said to the disciple, 'Behold, your mother!' And from that hour the disciple took her to his own home" (John 19:26-27).

There is nothing at the intersection of 14th and Euclid to mark the miraculous moment when the kinship model of Erlin's family shifted. Nothing to mark his mother's blunt and radical understanding of what makes a family. But the plain prayers of children and ordinary people have soaked the weedy park strip. The blood of a young man—who did many things wrong and struggled to do a few things right—anoints the place, like on a sacrificial altar.

Ownership vs. kinship. Bread alongside blood. Where do you go to see the gospel unfold? Is part of the role for Christians in the city simply one of interpreting the symbols and mythology of centralized power and its creation of powerlessness at its margins?

Chapter 4
Zoning and Land Use
in the City of God

Who'd have thought they were walking into light
if it weren't for the darkness dragging
from their heels? [61]
—Catherine Sasanov

For all the anti-images of cities found in the Bible, there is also a matrix of city images that fuelled several generations of utopian urban planners. This is the tradition that sees the city as the home of God; the earthly city as a reflection of the heavenly city; cities as the locus of healing and redemption for all the nations.

There are hints of this thread in the earliest texts. There are the "cities of refuge" that Moses was instructed to build (Numbers 35:6-34). Jerusalem is the "holy city" or the "city of God." Isaiah refers to Jerusalem as the "City of Righteousness, a Faithful City" (Isaiah 1:26).

The apostle Paul, architect of urban Christianity, uses the word *ekklesia* to describe a group of Jesus followers who gather for prayer and fellowship. This is the same word used by the Greeks to describe the gathering of people who directed the policy of a city, the urban planners. In Paul's symbolism, the first Christians were to be the urban planning committees for the New Jerusalem.

Once when I was out walking through the neighborhood I had an experience that taught me an important lesson about Paul. In the midst of a noon stroll to buy lunch at the local deli I got knocked to my knees and found myself splayed out on the sidewalk. The fall was swift. It was brutal. It hurt like hell. No … this wasn't a random act of inner-city violence. I just tripped, apparently over my own feet. I fell straight forward like a nine year old, scraping knees, shins, and palms. Was Paul this sore after getting knocked off his high horse? With aching shoulders, neck, and muscles only God knew were there?

In recounting the story, a friend told me of her own experience tripping over the sidewalk with much worse results—split lip, bloody forehead, a mess. As she lay face down in the cement a number of people passed her by. Perhaps they thought she was drunk or having a seizure or they figured someone else would deal with the problem. The one who did stop was an older, homeless, Latino man who didn't speak English. He asked her over and over in slurred Spanish if she was ok. Then he reached into a very dirty pocket and pulled out a semi-clean handkerchief to wipe her face. When the police arrived, they shooed him away thinking him a nuisance. My friend, however, recognized him for who he was—an attending angel, a sordid saint, the despised face of Jesus. Getting knocked to one's knees every once in awhile is probably a good thing. The world looks different when viewed from the ground up.

•••

I'm interested in reclaiming sacred space in cities. What happens if we hold our Bible studies on busy street corners with winos, prostitutes, and drug dealers hanging around the edges? How does this environment change our reading of the sacred stories?

On the second anniversary of the Iraq War, I attended a small prayer vigil on a corner like the one described above. A homeless man stood at the edge of our circle and began asking questions. I stepped aside to talk to him. As the conversation unfolded, I learned he was a veteran of the secret Central America wars of the 1980s. He'd been a grunt with the Marines in Panama, El Salvador, and Nicaragua. He told me, "That stuff we did down there really messed me up. Now I can't stand loud noise. I don't like to be closed up inside a building and I shake all the time. It's hard for me to concentrate very long on anything." He'd been several times over the years to the Veterans Administration hospital for help. "It's just a lot of paper shuffling and you have to have a phone for them to call you back to give you an appointment in three months," he said. "I finally just gave up."

Our public prayer service and his personal parable raised unexpected questions for me. What does it mean for a church to "adopt-a-block" —like the Catholic neighborhood parish model—and protect that delineated area with prayer sentinels? What implications might this have for local ministry, economy, and choice of location? What does the biblical precept of "sanctuary" mean for a church in a high-crime area? Can Isaiah's vision that "they shall neither hurt nor harm on all my holy mountain" have an urban version?

Many city neighborhoods have a prayer rhythm. Often it is indistinct and takes time and much watching to discern. But sometimes it jumps out at you. Back at the corner of 14th and Euclid Streets across from the Amoco station, I began to notice another prayer story. Many evenings at sunset during Ramadan, I observed the Domino's pizza deliveryman kneeling down to pray. About 50 years old, he wore dark pants, white high-top sneakers, and the pizza company's bright red shirt. In the dusty space between the cracked sidewalk and the asphalt, between the traffic light pole and a chipped green fire hydrant, he laid down a faded prayer rug and faced the rose-washed bricks of the Olympia apartment building toward the east.

This street corner is what historian of religion Mircea Eliade would call "profane space." It is homogenous; no place is more significant than another. There is no center to it. The Amoco station is physically the same as every other Amoco station. Late night patrons regularly hear rounds of gunshots and hit the ground. Cars run the stoplights—our symbols of order. The occasional shooting deaths complete the chaos.

Profane space is chaotic space, without shape or order. Profane space leads to a lack of reality; a dismantling of humanness. As the sun slanted behind him in the west, the Domino's deliveryman laid out his blue and tan prayer rug and removed his shoes. Perhaps he thinks this place is not as clean as it should be or mourns he is not with a community of believers. Perhaps he feels guilty that, with his work schedule, he cannot complete all the sunset prayers. Still, he touches his forehead to the ground.

At that moment of prayer, he is not simply one more object in the urban landscape. Rather he has become a hierophany—a disruption of profane space by the manifestation of the divine. His act of praying transforms the cityscape into sacred space, holy ground. Moses sees a burning bush. Mary sees an angel. What does the pizza man see?

Through his prayer, this inner-city intersection gains

a sacred center—an *axis mundi*. He becomes a meeting point between heaven and earth. Here the sacred world approaches the profane one, and our profane humanity may approach the sacred. He provides a point of orientation in space and time whereby the world beyond him may be shaped, ordered, and structured. Through his prayer practice, he transforms chaos into cosmos. He restores reality. He creates humanness. He incarnates. For a time, strangers become neighbors, a red light becomes a Sabbath moment, and the frenetic urban energy slows perceptibly around him.

The Hebrew scriptures often refer to sacred spaces. Abram and Sarai moved from Sichem to Bethel to the sacred oaks of Mamre in Hebron. The wilderness they passed through was aimless and nameless. It was non-place. Profane.

According to Eliade, every manifestation of the holy re-founds the world by bending back time to its sacred beginning. Each hierophany infuses time with the elemental joy present at creation. In doing so, this sacred experience becomes an antidote to the "terror of history"—the existential helplessness we feel before the crushing realities of historical time. For salvific religions this in-breaking returns the world to the moment of liberation, re-founding it in freedom.

The New Testament broke down the distinctions of sacred and profane. Not by abandoning all to profanity, but by extending the reach of sacred time and space. Jesus commanded the Sabbath, not the other way around, and his followers became the "living stones" of God's sacred temple, rather than unclean worshipers. Over the centuries of belief, those who were dispossessed become God-possessed; where they walk now may become holy ground. Like living cathedrals, their interior lives are ordered with a terrible beauty.

Domino's Pizza ("The Pizza Delivery Experts") didn't deliver to Columbia Heights until 2000. Too many of their drivers got robbed. Now, this Domino's deliveryman probably works 30 hours a week at this job. He might make $6.15 an hour and get $35 each night in tips. According to the National Low Income Housing Coalition, he'd have to make $23.92 an hour working more than full-time just to rent a modest two-bedroom home in the District of Columbia.[62] By all accounts, he's an ordinary man. And yet, what happens to the world when he kneels down to pray?

There are other kinds of worship that happen in public spaces, though they may not seem like any worship we recognize. For several years now I've been a back pew observer at the First Church of the Wax and Shine. It took me a little while to unravel the complexity and nuances of this particular denomination. Now, after a steady stream of low-key evangelization, I'm beginning to catch on.

Worship starts fashionably late on Sunday mornings—an hour that takes into account Saturday night. It happens on the street, or in the alley, or in the corner of a parking lot. It requires a vehicle (vintage or new), a comfortably clean chamois cloth, Turtle Wax, and a decent set of woofers. The radio volume is adjusted to a low window-rumbling volume and tuned to a local power preacher, or Kirk Franklin's Nu Nation, or Mary J. Blige.

When the groove is laid down nice and sweet then the steady meditative stroking of the ride begins. The hood, the wheel wells, the chrome. Like praying the rosary or making up a "church lady's" covered dish, there is a special mingling of the mystical and the mundane on Sunday mornings at the First Church of the Wax and Shine. O, Swing Low, Sweet Chariot … To a certain extent, this "church" is one of urban contemplatives. What are the prayer rhythms of your city?

•••

The last city images in the Bible are in the final book: Revelation. Finally, we come to John's most amazing vision as described in this often misunderstood and abused scripture—the City of God. Here we find images of received wisdom set completely in an urban context with urban symbols (not in the traditional wilderness location for receiving wisdom). John receives a blue print for the City of God that includes dimensions, the number of gates, their placement, the materials to be used, plumb lines, zoning regulations, and land use. The urban plan is geometric and based on celestial calculations just like the ancient cities, except the celestial bodies are now God and the Lamb: "The city does not need the sun or the moon to shine on it, for the glory of God gives it light, and the Lamb is its lamp" (Revelation 21:23).

This city in Revelation is not protected by military might. Its gates and fortifications are always open in an architectural gesture of hospitality: "Its gates will never be shut by day—and there will be no night there" (Revelation 21:25).

It is a radically "green" city with access to fresh water right in the middle of town: "Then the angel showed me the river of the water of life, bright crystal, flowing from the throne of God and of the Lamb through the middle of the street of the city" (Revelation 22:1).

It is a city that not only feeds its own people from the multi-fruit producing tree of life, but also offers health for the nations through the leaves of that tree: "On either side of the river is the tree of life with twelve kinds of fruit, producing its fruit each month; and the leaves of the tree are for the healing of the nations" (Revelation 22:2).

However, the fundamental difference between this city and all previous cities is at its core. All prior cities were organized to concentrate power in the center and to disempower the margins. The religious-political power was housed in the central Temple, which—architecturally and in every other way—dominated through force everything around it. From the Temple the political-religious power reached out and conquered people, land, and social structure through fear, force, and the demand for allegiance. The Temple housed the altar on which blood sacrifices— the bodies of children, the bodies of scapegoats—were required.

In John's vision of the new City of God, however, there is no Temple. "And I saw no temple therein," writes John the Revelator, "for the Lord God Almighty and the Lamb are the temple of it." There is no Temple in the glorious City of God because Temple worship has been replaced by the living presence of the Lamb of God.

The "empire" this city rules is not run by blood sacrifice. The nation with this city as its center does not require scapegoats or victims to operate. On the streets of *this* city in Revelation, nine-year-old Donte Manning's blood would not be poured out.

The Lamb in this city does not conquer and control through domination, military might, or economic exploitation. The Lamb in the city center does not victoriously rule over the empire's subjects. In fact, the most heart-rending characteristic about the Lamb is it is wounded and weak: "Then I saw between the throne and the four living creatures and among the elders a Lamb standing as if it had been slaughtered ..." (Revelation 5:6).

The blood of this vulnerable Lamb—or scapegoat—is a sign the system of sacrifice has been overcome. The broken and gutted body of the Lamb breaks the "mimetic cycle of violence," as anthropological philosopher René Girard describes it, of worldly empire. "The victory of Christ," Girard writes in *I See Satan Fall Like Lightning*, "has nothing to do with the military triumph of a victorious general: rather than inflicting violence on others, Christ submits to it." [63]

How does this vision of city in Revelation instruct us to live? Can we submit ourselves to this vision of city and *polis* and empire? Can we receive it and be instructed, discipled, by it—rather than imposing on it a particular utopian or dystopian model? How is human and community identity shaped in this city? Is it possible to have an experience of the urban that is not antithetical to land and the needs of the earth?

In the early 21st century, humankind reached a tipping

point. For the first time in human history, more people live in urban than rural areas—3.3 billion people worldwide.[64] "The arrival of *Homo urbanus*," writes United Nations Under-Secretary General Anna Tibaijuka, "could be a cause for celebration: For the first time in history, half of humanity lives in towns and cities. However, of this three billion people, one billion have little to celebrate."

What will the world look like in 2030? The global urban population will have reached 5 billion. Eighty percent of the global population will live in the Global South. Two billion people will live in the favelas, squatter villages, townships, and colonias that ring urban centers. Of the 23 cities expected to exceed a population of 10 million by 2015, 19 of them will be in the Global South, reports *The New Internationalist*.[65] What will *Homo urbanus* worship?

What does the urban blueprint presented in Revelation teach us about how to live now in the age of *Homo urbanus*, in an era of ecological collapse?

•••

On the western edge of my neighborhood in Columbia Heights there is a big park called Meridian Hill. It hangs precariously on the Fall Line of the eastern Piedmont Plateau. Two hundred feet above sea level, Meridian Hill is the lowest and final edge of this massive, ancient amalgam of metamorphic rock. The Fall Line is where the hard granite of the Appalachian mountains meets the soft silt of the Atlantic coastal plain. The last major geologic events to substantially alter this region were the final break-up of Pangaea 40 million years ago, when Eurasia and North America drifted apart, and the impact 35 million years ago of a an asteroid that hit near present-day Norfolk, Virginia, splashing mud and rock high into the atmosphere.

In Columbia Heights, all this geology translates into an amazing view—a natural high point from which to scan the wet lands of the Potomac in earlier days and now a vista on the Federal City. "Meridian Hill Park was named," reported Linda Wheeler in a 1981 *Washington Post* article,[66] "for the meridian stone marker placed by the city near 16th Street and Florida Avenue in 1791. Originally part of a large private estate, the federal government bought the land in 1910 and the park was completed in 1936."

The placement of the meridian stone was based on the celestial calculations and survey work of Benjamin Banneker. It marks the longitudinal line that, in the early 1800s, Thomas Jefferson hoped would become the first American prime meridian from which all future mapping would be accomplished. Jefferson's meridian ran through the White House and up 16th Street through Meridian Hill Park.

Now called Malcolm X Park by locals, Meridian Hill is a meeting place for city folks from all different cultures. Salvadorans, Bosnians, and Haitians don't share a language, but they all know how to play soccer. And the field is almost always in use.

On Sunday afternoon in the center of the park there is a drumming circle. About 40 drummers gather with about 100 onlookers. It's been going on for at least 35 years. They are often joined by members of a professional Nigerian dance troupe who are overjoyed to dance in a public space rather than on a stage for "entertainment."

This drum and dance circle is a place where people pray with their bodies. They shout out praise. They cry and comfort one another. There is a woman who stands off to the side holding out burning incense. She blesses those who come to her, sometimes including healing touch. There are little kids and elders; gang-bangers and "suits." There are Rasta guardians who let newcomers know that marijuana and alcohol should not be brought into the circle. People share their picnics with each other; they feed the birds, and put out bowls of water for dogs. When asked why she came here every week, one woman responded, "I need this on Sundays to carry me through Monday." To me, this drumming circle, high on the Piedmont Fall Line, looks like John's City of God.

•••

Donte Manning's grandmother attends Mass at Immaculate Conception Catholic Church, where I also attend. The priest there, Fr. Watkins, has dedicated himself to serving this very poor African-American congregation and helping it survive the vicissitudes of gentrification. (His father was Chief of Naval Operations during the Reagan Administration and Secretary of Energy under President George H. W. Bush.)

Donte's mother and stepfather attend Shiloh Baptist Church around the corner from Immaculate Conception. The funeral for Donte was held at Shiloh with Fr. Watkins and Shiloh's pastor Thomas Bowen presiding. More than 500 people attended, including Donte's third-grade classmates. A column of white carnations next to the altar spelled out the word "Innocence."

Then-Washington, D.C. mayor Anthony A. Williams spoke at the service. He called the death "a reflection of our own communities." Donte's teacher, Carol Young, said she and Donte had reversed roles recently when he taught her a lesson. Donte, Young said, was having trouble with a couple of students, and she told him he might need to stand up for himself. "Ms. Young, that's just not me," Donte told her. "I don't fight."

As a Christian acting and operating on an urban stage, I ask again: Where are the bodies? Whose blood is sacrificed on whose altar and for what purpose? How is Donte Manning's blood—shed on a Washington, D.C., sidewalk— also Christ's blood?

I'll posit this in conclusion. In Christian imagination, the sacrificial dynamic began when God created us out of God's own body. Sacrifice begins with God, not us. It is a freely given offering of self made in love for the other. It is not coerced. What is the appropriate response to God's action? "The radical self-offering of the faithful is the only spiritual response that constitutes an authentic sacrificial act ...," cites Jesuit Robert Daly in an essay on liturgy and sacrifice. Jesus asks for love, not sacrifice.[67]

Donte Manning did not freely give his life in sacrifice. His life was taken from him by the "agents of sacrifice," as Rene Girard puts it, for purposes of revenge.

However, as Christians, it is our work to make holy Donte's sacrifice. We do this by gathering as believers and begging the Holy Spirit to sanctify the body and blood of this boy.

What happens when we do this? First, we reinterpret our ancient memory into a contemporary setting thus maintaining its authenticity. Second, we proclaim our

Christian belief that "death no longer has dominion" (Romans 6:9)—specifically that the forces of death that seek to rule our world have been subverted from the beginning and we will continue to remind them of this weakness. Third, our identity as disciples of Jesus is strengthened, our body of Christ made stronger, through claiming this boy's death as "eucharistic." "Eucharistic real presence is not for its own sake," says Robert Daly, "but for the purpose of the eschatological transformation of the participants." [68]

To live as a Christian in my neighborhood where this event took place and not to witness it with the fullness of my religious imagination would mean not only to abandon Donte to a meaningless death, but also to blaspheme the eucharistic sacrifice. To refuse to witness would erode the power for me of what happens on the altar on Sundays. As a disciple of Jesus, I must adopt habits of living that allow Donte's death to transform me in radical ways. If I don't take on the virtues of a boy who says to his teacher "I don't fight," then I interrupt the fullness of the eucharistic event.

Nearly two years after Donte was killed, I noticed new flyers put up by the Metropolitan Police Department in the Amoco Station at 14th and Euclid. The reward stands at $125,000. Donte's murder remains unsolved.

Epilogue

You don't have anything if you don't have the stories.
—Leslie Marmon Silko, *Ceremony* [69]

Since completing this book, readers have asked two particular questions: What happened to Donte Manning's family and what do you hope to achieve by writing this book?

To the first I must say I know very little. Donte was buried in a Catholic cemetery on the outskirts of D.C. and his family moved away from the Warner Apartments. Donte's murder officially has been designated a "cold case." In 2008, the D.C. Department of Corrections released a deck of "cold case playing cards." Donte's image and information about his murder are printed on the five of diamonds. The police hope by distributing decks of cold case cards to inmates in the D.C. jail, they will turn up information about Donte's murder.

Throughout the writing, I have been very conscious of my responsibilities in bearing witness—unasked—to a story not my own. Where I have done it imperfectly, I ask forgiveness—especially from Donte's family. Where I have succeeded, I offer that creative spark back to Donte's family for their loss and to the people of Columbia Heights, for their humanity.

To the second question of what I hope to achieve in this writing, I have several answers. Foremost, I want this book to point toward truth and unmask deception. I want Donte Manning's killer to come forward so that Donte's family can have justice and the person who killed him can retain some part of his humanity by accepting responsibility for his disastrous actions. (Witnesses say it was a young man.) A book, of course, can not elicit a confession. But by lifting up Donte's name and witnessing to the deeper truths and sacrifices involved in his life and death—and the life and death of Columbia Heights—perhaps I can do my part to help realize that "the arc of the moral universe is long but it bends toward justice," as Dr. Martin Luther King put it.

Additionally, I want this book to tear away the mask of myth that accompanies any age of empire. I needed to tell the story of my neighborhood through the ancient biblical stories. Not because I think the contemporary stories need to be bolstered by "Bible speak" religiosity. Quite the contrary. It's because I have entrusted my whole life to these biblical stories. It is through them I mature as a full human being, therefore it was only through the biblical lens I could read truly the stories of the streets. The difference between the biblical lens and the lens of myth, writes Rene Girard, is the "difference between a world where arbitrary violence triumphs without being recognized and a world where this same violence is identified, denounced, and finally forgiven. It's the difference between truth and deception… ."[70]

On a more creative note, I hope this way of crafting a "theology of place" will inspire and teach others to do the same. Our lives are rich with stories that mostly are stolen from us. It is only by remembering our stories we can reclaim our true selves. What are the stories under our feet, on the path we take to work, unfolding outside our kitchen window? What questions can we ask together about the place and the history of where we live, the lives that have passed through where we now are, the earth beneath our place, the wind and light surrounding it? What are our place's sacred stories and how can they ease our loneliness and fortify our vivaciousness?

For me, this kind of storytelling is part of the Christian's apostolic calling. The apostle Paul defined the apostolic life, in Romans 15, using the words *leitourgos* (public servant) and *hierourgein* (one who defends the sanctity of the law by undergoing violent death). This way of life is priestly, public, eschatological, and universal. It allows us to recognize and engage the interpretive space in which we live.

The priestly and public aspects of any Christian life are lived out in real time, ministering to real people. The eschatological and universal aspects are developed by exercising our Christian sense of time, recognizing the *kairos* moments amidst the daily and by listening, pondering, interpreting, reclaiming, and proclaiming the symbolic life of the people among whom we live in the place where we find ourselves. Stories, writes Leslie Marmon Silko, "aren't just entertainment. Don't be fooled. They are all we have, you see, to fight off illness and death. You don't have anything if you don't have your stories." [71]

Endnotes

[1]"A Distinctly American Internationalism," by Gov. George W. Bush (presidential campaign speech given November 19, 1999) *The George W. Bush Foreign Policy Reader* edited by John W. Dietrich (M.E. Sharpe, 2005)

[2]"Faith, Certainty and the Presidency of George W. Bush," by Ron Suskind (*New York Times Magazine*, 2004-10-17)

[3]"The Mosquito and the Hammer: A Tomdispatch Interview with James Carroll" (11 September 2005).

[4]*The Prolific and the Devourer* by W.H. Auden (Hopewell, NJ: Ecco, 1976), p. 37-38.

[5]Eminem, J-Black & Masta Ace (2002). Hellbound. On *Hellbound* [Limited Edition CDS].

[6]"Radbertus & Ratramnus: A Ninth Century Debate over the Lord's Supper" by Shane Rosenthal (Reformation Ink; www.markers.com/ink).

[7]ibid

[8]"On the Heights," by Julie Polter. Unpublished essay.

[9]ibid

[10]National Register of Historic Places [http://www.nationalregisterofhistoricplaces.com/DC/District+of+Columbia/state.html]

[11]"Columbia Heights, Washington, D.C. 1904" (The Columbia Historical Society), p. 16.

[12]Private correspondence. E-mail from Larry Bellinger and Fran Bellinger to author on May 6, 2005.

[13]ibid

[14]*The Gift: Imagination and the Erotic Life of Property* by Lewis Hyde (Random House, 1983).

[15]"Anarchism," *Encyclopedia of Religion and Nature*, edited by Bron Taylor (Continuum, 2005).

[16]*The Beginnings of Desire* by Avivah Gottlieb Zornberg (Doubleday, 1995), p. 21.

[17]*The Meaning of the City* by Jacques Ellul (Wm. B. Eerdmans, 1970), p. 5-6.

[18]ibid

[19]"Discerning the Angel of Detroit" by Bill Kellermann (*Sojourners* October 1989, pp 16-21)

[20]NBC 4 News, April 21, 2005 [http://www.nbc4.com/news/4401177/detail.html]

[21]"Purity of the French Language," by Raymond Cho (Phi Beta Kappa Newsletters, Vol. 1, Number 1, February 2000.

[22]"The Fall," by Ched Myers, *Encyclopedia of Religion and Nature*, ed. Bron Taylor (2005).

[23]*Ancient Times, From Stone To Steel* by Robert A. Guisepi (International Civilization Press 2004) .

[24]"The Connection Between Religion and Urban Planning" by David Engwicht (Source: www.lesstraffic.com)

[25] *Babylon is Everywhere: The City as Man's Fate* by Wolf Schneider (McGraw-Hill, 1963)

[26]ibid

[27] "The Connection Between Religion and Urban Planning" by David Engwicht (Source: www.lesstraffic.com)

[28]"The Vision of Pierre L'Enfant: A City to Inspire, A Plan to Preserve" by Glen Worthington (Georgetown Law Historic Preservation Papers Series, 2005), p. 6.

[29]"A Public Museum of Trees: Mid-Nineteenth Century Plans for the Mall," by Therese O'Malley in The Mall in Washington 1791-1991 (Richard Longstreth, ed.) Hanover: University Press of New England, 1991.

[30]"Civil War Defenses of Washington," National Park Service, U.S. Department of Interior (October 02, 2007).

[31]"U.S. Army airship missions over the Washington DC metro area, Maryland and Northern Virginia," Army Public Affairs News Release (September 22, 2004).

[32]"Congress Approves $2.6 Trillion Budget," *Washington Times* (April 29, 2005)

[33]"2006 Federal Budget Year in Review," National Priorities Project.

[34]"Low-Income Children in the United States: National and State Trend Data 1996-2006," National Center for Children in Poverty.

[35]"Births: Final Data for 2004," (National Vital Statistics Report, Vol. 55, Number 1).

[36]"2006 American Community Survey: R1701," U.S. Census Bureau.

[37]"Hobbling a Generation: Young African American Men in Washington, D.C.'s Criminal Justice System—Five Years Later" by Eric Lotke (*Crime & Delinquency*, Vol. 44, No. 3, 355-366, 1998)

[38]"Patterns of Concentrated Neighborhood Poverty" Chapter 7, *Housing in the Nation's Capital* (Fannie Mae Foundation, 2003).

[39]*The Sphinx in the City: Urban Life, the Control of Disorder, and Women* by Elizabeth Wilson (University of California Press, 1992, p. 5).

[40]"Patterns of Concentrated Neighborhood Poverty" Chapter 7, Housing in the Nation's Capital (Fannie Mae Foundation, 2003)

[41]"Appendix B, Table B1," Housing in the Nation's Capital (Fannie Mae Foundation, 2003), http://www.fanniemaefoundation.org/publications/reports/hnc/2003/pdf/HNC03_EndMatter.pdf

[42]Unpublished research for "On the Heights," by Julie Polter.

[43]Washington DC Recorder of Deeds, public records, 2005.

[44]"Boy Shot While Playing in Northwest," by Clarence Williams and Allan Lengel, (*The Washington Post*, March 25, 2005).

[45]"2002 Annual Assessment of Cocaine Movement," Office of National Drug Control Policy (March 2003)

[46]*Binding the Strong Man* by Ched Myers (Orbis, 1990), p.103.

[47]*Moby-Dick* by Herman Melville (Penguin, 1992), Chapter 37.

[48]"Kids in the Crosshairs," by Rose Marie Berger (*Sojourners*, February 2005); author's own research.

[49]*Schools for Conversion: 12 Marks of a New Monasticism* by Margaret McKenna (Cascade House: 2005).

[50]"Wounded D.C. Boy, 9, Loses Fight For Life," by Del Quentin Wilber and Petula Dvorak (*The Washington Post*, April 27, 2005).

[51]*Moby-Dick* by Herman Melville (Penguin, 1992), Chapter 109.

[52]Starbucks Company Profile (February 2008).

[53]"At Work; Benefits? For Part-Timers?" by Barbara Presley Noble (*New York Times*, August 16, 1992).

[54]"A Hot Year for Coffee?" by Carolyn Whelan. *International Herald Tribune* (March 19, 2005).

[55]"Dead or Alive: Hunting Osama bin Laden" by Mary Louise Kelly. "Morning Edition" National Public Radio, May 2, 2005.

[56]"Dealing with the Coffee Crisis in Central America: Impacts and Strategies" by Panos Varangis, Paul Siegel, Daniele Giovannucci, Bryan Lewin (World Bank Policy Research Working Paper #2993, March 2003, section 142).

[57]"Coffee Production in El Salvador" (www.hasbean.co.uk) http://www.hasblog.co.uk/?p=164#comment-20732

[58]El Salvador statistics http://ksghome.harvard.edu/~rhausma/elsvdr/salvadoransoversea.pdf

[59]"Holding Their Ground in Columbia Heights" by Sylvia Moreno (*The Washington Post*, December 9, 2007).

[60]"Planning and Placemaking as a form of Fundamentalism," by David Engwicht (1999) www.lesstraffic.com.

[61] "At the Restoration of Massacio's *Fresco The Expulsion of Adam and Eve*," *All the Blood Tethers* by Catherine Sasanov (Boston: Northeastern University Press, 2002), p. 32.

[62]"Updated Congressional District Profiles" (June 12, 2008) http://www.nlihc.org/doc/cdpDC.pdf

[63]*I See Satan Fall Like Lightning* by René Girard (Gracewing Publishing, 2001), p. 140.

[64]"Tomorrow's Crises Today: The Humanitarian Impact of Urbanization" (OCHA/IRIN and U.N.-HABITAT, September 2007).

[65]"Urban Explosion: The Facts," *The New Internationalist* (January 2006, Issue 386).

[66]Dark Side of a Park," by Linda Wheeler (*The Washington Post,* Aug. 30, 1981).

[67]"Sacrifice Unveiled or Sacrifice Revisited: Trinitarian and Liturgical Perspectives," by Robert Daly, SJ, *Theological Studies 64* (2003), pp. 27–28.

[68]Personal correspondence and further developed in "Sacrifice Unveiled or Sacrifice Revisited: Trinitarian and Liturgical Perspectives," by Robert Daly, SJ, *Theological Studies 64* (2003), pp. 27–28.

[69]*Ceremony,* by Leslie Marmon Silko (Penguin, 1986), p. 2.

[70]*I See Satan Fall Like Lightning* by René Girard (Gracewing Publishing, 2001), p. 144.

[71]*Ceremony*, by Leslie Marmon Silko (Penguin, 1986), p. 2.

Reader's Guide

In *Who Killed Donte Manning?* author Rose Marie Berger uses three essential elements to develop a "theology of place": the Washington, D.C. neighborhood of Columbia Heights, the Bible, and the economic, social, and political tides from beyond the neighborhood that influence the lives of those within it. Berger examines how Judeo-Christian images and values have influenced urban life and urban architecture, while at the same time exploring a contemporary living faith found among people on the streets of an inner-city American neighborhood. She uses biblical imagery to both indict the way the urban experiment fails to foster human dignity and champion the stories of individuals who crack through the architecture of despair to claim their humanity.

Who Killed Donte Manning? is a perfect entre for neighborhood groups who want to experiment with the "theology of place," to learn more about the history and life of their own locale, to understand the outside forces that shape their region, and ultimately gain deeper understanding of the myths and stories that give meaning to the place they call home.

Introduction

Berger describes a project that uncovered the history of her 100-year-old row house in Columbia Heights, Washington, D.C.

■ What do you know about the history of the land and geography, house or apartment, and tenants over time in the place where you live?

■ Berger says that "our perspective is shaped by what we see out the window every morning when we wake up." What does she mean? What do you see from your window? What do you *not* see? How does your window view shape the kinds of social and political questions you ask?

Chapter 1

The story of the death of nine-year-old Donte Manning frames Berger's narrative. She interprets this death through her Catholic lens of the seasons of the church year. Additionally, she examines biblical anti-city images that are foundational to the book of Genesis and examines the location of the altar—the place of sacrifice—in American cities.

■ Why is it significant to Berger that Donte Manning was shot during Holy Week?

■ Berger asks the provocative question: "Who lives, who dies, and why?" in Columbia Heights. How would you ask this for your own locale? What would the local newspaper's obituaries tell you? Whose life stories are not included in those obits?

■ Have you examined the biblical images of the city in Genesis before? Do you agree with Berger there is an anti-urban bias? Why? How might this have shaped the way some Christians view the city and urban-dwellers as in particular need of "salvation"?

■ Berger connects the story in Genesis of Cain and Abel with the shooting of Donte Manning through the question God asks Cain: "Where is your brother?" (Genesis 4:9). Would you describe this way of thinking as a literalist interpretation of the Bible? What is Berger's goal in reading scripture—and her neighborhood—this way?

Chapter 2

Berger explains how Washington, D.C., was designed along lines similar to ancient biblical cities. Drawing on the history of the region, she examines the military fortifications of Washington both pre- and post-Sept. 11. Tracking the forces that exert pressure on the Columbia Heights, Berger uses a trip she took to Colombia to trace the drug trade that lead to the death of Donte Manning.

■ What is the layout of the city or town where you live? What does the design plan emphasize? What does it discourage? Who does it bring together or divide?

■ How has your city or neighborhood changed since Sept. 11? Have security measures changed? Have those changes resulted in increased security? Who has been most disadvantaged by post-Sept. 11 changes?

■ What forces exert the most pressure on your town or neighborhood? If you mapped your local economic "tides," where would the money or resources flow? What gets bypassed or diverted?

■ Berger traces the "story lines" of her neighborhood. She identifies characters, plots and sub-plots, tensions, set in an historical timeline. In what ways is this an effective approach? What information does it leave out?

Chapter 3

In the opening of *Who Killed Donte Manning?*, Berger includes three quotes about the nature of empire—a government or business that has expanded its territory or economic control over populations distinct from itself by use of force. Chapter 3 expands on these three quotes by looking closely at how the mechanics of the American Empire—from Starbucks, to Iraq, to El Salvador—function in Columbia Heights. Berger also shares intimate stories about a bread delivery man who can't give bread and a mother adopting her son's "crew."

■ What is "gentrification"? How does it function? Who does it benefit? Who loses?

■ The Youth Action Resource Group in Columbia Heights is a youth-driven media and organizing project in Washington, D.C., that supports teenagers in creating their own media, doing research on their neighborhood, and building social and political analysis. Why does Berger consider this perspective important? How does an organization like YARG encourage democratic ideals?

■ Coffee and oil are two of the highest traded commodities. What do these products have to do with empire or imperial expansion? How does Berger relate this to Columbia Heights? How does it relate to your neighborhood or town?

■ What are the biblical critiques of those who build empires? Are there biblical narratives that appear to support the building of empires? What role do the biblical prophets have in assessing economies, military might, and the power of religious authorities?

■ Why are the stories Berger shares about the Wonder Bread truck driver and the prayer service for Uncle Erlin important? What relationship do they have to the concept of empire?

Chapter 4

The last chapter explores the positive biblical images of the city, especially as they relate to the "City of God" in the book of Revelation. As counter-point to Chapter 1, Berger identifies the radically new understanding of the temple and the altar in the City of God and examines what "sacred space" looks like in Columbia Heights. She asks how *Homo urbanus* will worship in the future.

■ What is unique in Berger's interpretation of the City of God in Revelation? How does it compare with other interpretations of Revelation you may have heard?

■ Why does she call Revelation's City of God a "radically 'green' city"? Why is the environmental component important? How is the City of God different from the imperial or ancient cities identified at the beginning of the book?

■ Berger began in Chapter 1 with the concept of sacrifice and the altar. Where does she end up?

■ What are the elements of liturgy described in the Drumming Circle in Meridian Hill/Malcolm X Park? What does this gathering lack in terms of religious worship? How does it compare to the experience of "church" in a typical Sunday-morning Christian service?

■ Why does she say it was important to her to explore Donte Manning's murder?

Epilogue

Berger addresses questions that have been raised by readers and encourages groups to explore their own "theology of place."

■ Do you think of yourself has having a "ministry" or "gift" that you offer freely to the people in your neighborhood for the betterment of their lives? What values undergird this way of thinking?

■ She interprets Donte Manning's death through a Christian lens. How might she have told this story and interpreted these events through the lens of Islam or Judaism?

Bibliography and Selected Reading

Babylon is Everywhere: The City as Man's Fate by Wolf Schneider (McGraw-Hill, 1963)

The Beginning of Desire: Reflections on Genesis by Avivah Gottlieb Zornberg (Image, 1996)

Binding the Strong Man: A Political Reading of Mark's Story of Jesus by Ched Myers (Orbis Books, 1990)

A Christian Theology of Place: Explorations in Practical, Pastoral, and Empirical Theology by John Inge (Ashgate Publishing, Ltd., 2003)

Constantine's Sword: The Church and the Jews: A History by James Carroll (Houghton Mifflin, 2001)

The Edges of the Field: Lessons on the Obligations of Ownership by Joseph William Singer (Beacon Press, 2000)

First In: An Insider's Account of How the CIA Spearheaded the War on Terror in Afghanistan by Gary C. Schroen (Random House, 2005)

The Gift: Imagination and the Erotic Life of Property by Lewis Hyde (Trafalgar Square, 1999)

GIS: Geographic Information Systems for the Social Sciences: Investigating Space and Place by Steven J. Steinberg and Sheila L. Steinberg (Sage Publications Inc, 2006)

Goatwalking: A Guide to Wildland Living by Jim Corbett (Viking Press, 1991)

Guerrilla Gardening: A Manualfesto by David Tracey (New Society Publishers, 2007)

I See Satan Fall Like Lightning by René Girard (Orbis Books, 2001)

The Meaning of the City by Jacques Ellul (Wm. B. Eerdmans, 1970)

On Guerrilla Gardening: A Handbook for Gardening Without Boundaries by Richard Reynolds (Bloomsbury USA, 2008)

Past Time, Past Place: GIS for History edited by Anne Kelly Knowles (ESRI, 2001)

Remotely Sensed Cities by Victor Mesev (Taylor & Francis, Inc, 2003)

The Sacred and the Profane: The Nature of Religion by Mircea Eliade (Harcourt Brace Jovanovich, 1959)

Sanctuary for All Life: The Cowbalah of Jim Corbett (edited by Daniel Baker; Howling Dog Press, 2005)

Shopping Malls and Other Sacred Spaces: Putting God in Place by Jon Pahl (Brazos, 2003)

The Sphinx in the City: Urban Life, the Control of Disorder, and Women by Elizabeth Wilson (University of California Press, 1992)

Street Reclaiming: Creating Livable Streets and Vibrant Communities by David Engwicht (Published by New Society Publishers, 1999)

Credits

Map by Jackie Spycher (2008)

Author photograph by Rick Reinhard

Acknowledgments

With deepest gratitude to: Barbara and John Berger; Howard and Kate Auble; Gage, Joe, Michelle, Sorelle and Zev Berger; the students of Apprentice House; Karen Lattea; Ched Myers; Joseph Ross; Helene Slesserev-Jamir; Solea; Heidi Thompson; Steve Thorngate; Gregg Wilhelm; and Bill Wylie-Kellermann. I want to especially thank my friend, co-worker, and house co-owner Julie Polter, who has done a tremendous amount of research into the history of Columbia Heights and into the history of our house and who also gave invaluable editing help on this manuscript. Additionally, I give thanks for all the souls that have inhabited and will inhabit the Home of the Bottomless Cup on Fairmont Street.

About the Author

Rose Marie Berger is a Catholic peace activist and writer. She is a longtime associate editor at the award-winning progressive magazine *Sojourners* (www.sojo.net) and a regular columnist on spirituality, nonviolence, poetry, and social justice. Berger is the author of the books *Syllables of the Perfect Word* and co-editor of *Cut Loose the Body: An Anthology of Poems on Torture*. Her articles on faith communities working for peace in situations of war and violence have taken her to Belfast, Bosnia, Colombia, Kosovo, and El Salvador. Berger has an MFA in poetry from Stonecoast at the University of Southern Maine and lives in the Columbia Heights neighborhood of Washington, D.C., with her dog Solea. She can be reached at www.rosemarieberger.com.

Apprentice House is the country's only campus-based, student-staffed book publishing company. Directed by professors and industry professionals, it is a nonprofit activity of the Communication Department at Loyola University Maryland.

Using state-of-the-art technology and an experiential learning model of education, Apprentice House publishes books in untraditional ways. This dual responsibility as publishers and educators creates an unprecedented collaborative environment among faculty and students, while teaching tomorrow's editors, designers, and marketers.

Outside of class, progress on book projects is carried forth by the AH Book Publishing Club, a co-curricular campus organization supported by Loyola University's Office of Student Activities.

Student Project Team for *Who Killed Donte Manning?*:

    Kathleen Boehl, '11
    Kathleen Baumer, '10
    Caitlin Sullivan, '08
    Mike Tirone, '08

To learn more about Apprentice House books or to obtain submission guidelines, please visit www.apprenticehouse.com.

Apprentice House
Communication Department
Loyola University Maryland
4501 N. Charles Street
Baltimore, MD 21210
Ph: 410-617-5265
info@apprenticehouse.com